Advance Praise

"*The PatternShift* is another smash hit by Dr. T, giving all of us another shot at bringing more luxurious intentionality into our lives in the simplest, easiest way."

—DR. NYEISHA DEWITT,
Founder and CEO of ONGB

"*The PatternShift* is a masterpiece that will surely transform millions of lives. Dr. T's teachings on how to patternshift your reality are breathtaking as they bring you into a higher echelon of life that is pure luxury."

—TERROON KIBWE,
actor and producer

"Changing patterns may sound hard, but it actually isn't with this advice. Do yourself a favor and read this life-changing book!"

—CAROLINE KALENTZOS,
Influencer and CEO of Posh PR

"Dr. T has done it again! Like her previous titles, *The PatternShift* is wise, entertaining, and easy to implement."

**—HILARY SILVER,
love and relationship coach, Founder and CEO of the Hillary Silver Coaching Company**

"A potent invitation to actively participate in the evolution, elevation, and amplification of your life, love, and business."

**—ROB GROVER and GARY LOGAN,
Founders of The Journeymen Collective**

THE
PATTERNSHIFT™

THE
PATTERNSHIFT™

TRANSFORM YOUR REALITY
THROUGH INTENTIONALITY

DR. TRACY THOMAS

Copyright © 2023 Tracy Thomas
All rights reserved.

The PatternShift™
Transform Your Reality Through Intentionality

ISBN: 978-1-5445-3932-4 Hardcover
         978-1-5445-3933-1 Paperback
         978-1-5445-3934-8 Ebook

The Patternshift™ *is dedicated to
one of the most important contributors to my life:
the one and only Mr. Tony Robbins.*

*Quite simply, Tony is a world-class PatternShifter
who has dedicated his life to helping the world transform
their lives through shifting their patterns and
stepping into their next level lives.*

*The first time I saw Tony on an infomercial,
I was captivated and willing to buy whatever he was selling,
because he was so compelling. He was profoundly different
from anyone I'd ever seen in this life, and he helped me
feel that it was okay to be unique, confident, and powerful,
and that it was okay to live out my purpose and live
it out loud. Tony showed me that there are other dedicated
people who are doing all they can to elevate our society, and
this has given me great comfort in a world where everyone
needs to wake up and live out their destiny.*

*As I've followed Tony throughout his trajectory,
I've recognized a soul brother speaking the exact same language
of my mind and heart and yet with his unique "Tony-ness."
To have Tony share the wisdom that flows through him
and be so definitive in energy, language, tone, clarity, and
his strong views on reality has given me great peace
and prosperity. In short, he's made it okay for my purpose
and my destiny to be my number-one priority.*

*Tony's years of dedication to our world and helping
people shape their reality has shown me that there is a
"Reality Family" that I connect with at a deeper level in this
world. He's shown me that I am in the greatest company
of powerful leaders who say what needs to be said and
do what needs to be done. Tony has taught me
how to "burn the boats," making my most
intentional future the only option.*

*Each time I've gotten to engage with Tony,
I've found myself nodding my head, smiling, and laughing,
knowing there are people just like me who care deeply about
waking people up to their potential, people who are needed to
lead in this world. Because of Tony, I've developed a greater
confidence in my purpose and a validation of what it*

means to be "all in" for a whole new paradigm of an intentional reality that elevates everybody.

The era of Tony Robbins has made it possible for transformation to be both my obsession and my occupation, and the new paradigm that Tony has brought forth makes it possible for my intentional reality dynasty to fully expand. To be able to develop the world's first intentional reality company is possible because of the prolific presence of Tony and everything he has done for humanity.

There are millions of leaders, doctors, trainers, authors, and coaches, all trying to elevate the world with their words, deeds, suggestions, and solutions. There are millions of influencers putting everything they have into the world, helping us all to make the shift into a new reality and embrace who we really are and what we came here to do. Then there is the ever-presence of Tony Robbins, a giant of generosity and a constant voice for the transformation of humanity. It is his presence and seeing him live out his destiny that has inspired me to make The Patternshift *available for my human family.*

Contents

Foreword | xiii
SHAWN HARPER

Introduction | 1

Understanding Patterns | 11

PatternShift 1 | 29
UNCONSCIOUS TO CONSCIOUS

PatternShift 2 | 41
DISCONNECTED TO CONNECTED

PatternShift 3 | 55
NEGATIVE TO POSITIVE

PatternShift 4 | 67
REACTION TO INTENTION

PatternShift 5 | 81
BACKWARD TO FORWARD

PatternShift 6 | 93
PROTECTION TO MOMENTUM

PatternShift 7 | 107
FICTIONAL TO FACTUAL

PatternShift 8 | 117
PAIN TO PURPOSE

PatternShift 9 | 129
RELATIONSHIPS TO PARTNERSHIPS

PatternShift 10 | 143
SCARCITY TO LUXURY

Conclusion | 157

Further Resources | 161

Acknowledgments | 165

Foreword

SHAWN HARPER

Former NLF player, motivational speaker,
founder and CEO of Shawn Speaks,
and author of *The Winning Edge*

Even when you've reached the top level of your profession, you are probably still not operating at even a fraction of your full capacity. I'm a perfect example of this.

In the 1990s, I played in the National Football League (NFL) as an offensive tackle for the Los Angeles Rams and Indianapolis Colts. I also played for three years in NFL Europe, in Amsterdam and Frankfurt.

Foreword

But once I stopped playing football professionally, I had to reinvent myself. Although I found a second career I loved as a motivational speaker, the way I was thinking—my patterns—were holding me back from true success and happiness.

These patterns were insidious because they were hiding in ambiguity. They were buried in my subconscious, and I had no idea they were happening. My health, finances, and relationships were all suffering, and I couldn't understand why.

The most important patternshifts I've made have to do in the area of relationships. First, how I view myself in relationships: I had to move from victim to victor. When I did, all of my relationships greatly improved, including becoming a better husband and father.

In the area of finances, I was stuck in a rut for years, charging the same rate for my services. More recently, I made a change in my mind and heart to value myself more. It sent out these signals into the atmosphere, and the universe responded to me—I'm now charging the price point for my speaking engagements that I want to, which is incredibly empowering.

These patternshifts are all covered in the book you're about to read. They affect all of us, from all walks of life. And as potent as these patterns can be, you do have the power to change them. But you have to go into your subconscious and reprogram them.

I first met Dr. Tracy in 2020 when I was a guest on her YouTube show, "Elevate Your Life," and we talked about how to have a winning edge in life. This includes, of course, changing the patterns that are keeping you from the wins you want. We instantly connected and have been in touch in the years since our initial meeting.

Dr. Tracy has successfully helped countless clients shift the patterns that aren't working for them, and it's my sincere belief that if you follow the advice in this book, you can shift yours, too.

There isn't a lot of material out there about this subject, which is shocking to me. Patterns affect us every minute of every day, but most people don't understand them, let alone talk about them.

Foreword

I love this book because it actually pulls the cloak off of the subconscious. It teaches you how to recognize patterns and change them. That, in itself, is phenomenal.

It's well-established that most of our character and personality is developed by the age of seven. Oftentimes as we get older, we may feel helpless to change, like we're trapped in certain conditions. But as you learn how you can directly impact your subconscious, you can slowly change over time, no matter what your age. And I think that is the most liberating aspect of this book.

First, you choose, then you change, then you turn.

Read on to find out how to shift your patterns for good, allowing you to win on every field of life.

Introduction

Let's talk about patterns.

Think of the morning you had today—what kinds of patterns did you follow? For starters, you may have set an alarm clock to wake you. You probably brushed your teeth, using the same motions you always use to brush them. Maybe you drank a cup of coffee, put on your favorite pair of shoes, and closed the garage door as you left the house for work. As you drove to the office, you might have thought about what you need to get done.

Nothing is inherently right or wrong with any of these patterns.

Introduction

A pattern is the regular, repeated way something occurs. That can be the way something is done, the way it's said, or the way it's heard. The more it gets repeated, the more it becomes ingrained. A pattern builds momentum and keeps going unless something challenges it.

That's what can make a pattern so incredibly hard to break. In fact, we don't actually *break* patterns. More accurately, we *shift* them into something else.

I've observed and helped countless people over the years, and although every one of them was unique, I see some key patterns that keep people trapped in a life of stress and struggle. The truth is many of these patterns are errors. We think they are necessary, and they simply are not.

I'll show you how to recognize these dysfunctional patterns—and turn them into something you can use as your greatest advantage in life. The truth is that in order to be truly successful, this pattern is absolutely essential.

Some of your strongest patterns are those you were born into—genetics. In your genes are the many patterns of your biological parents' families. There are physical patterns, such as eye color, but we are primarily interested in the emotional patterns you've inherited. Zen Buddhists call this your *karmic package*—the emotional patterns that stretch back generations, not necessarily caused by you, but that can affect you nonetheless.[1]

One of the most pervasive patterns in our society is a pattern of scarcity. We inherited this from our ancestors because, going way back in time, life truly *was* about struggle and lack. Humans had to forage for food, hunt animals for meat, and be at the mercy of crop patterns and weather changes.

In modern times, we carry this stressful pattern with us, even though we are living in an era of abundance that would have been unfathomable to our ancestors. We can go to grocery stores stocked with food and take those groceries home to refrigerate and then cook on a stove. In fact, we have so much food that some of it is often wasted and thrown out. Scarcity is rarely a problem anymore.

---

[1] Powervie, "The Karmic Package," *Yorktown Zen* (blog), September 2, 2018, http://www.yorktownzen.org/blog/the-karmic-package.html.

Introduction

But we also take this mentality into other areas of our lives, especially finances. We live in a culture obsessed with making and having money, and yet we are saddled by a feeling of lack around the subject of money. People say they want to be financially successful, but they are often stuck in patterns of scarcity that keep them from the very success they desire.

For starters, most people are conditioned to believe they can have money and financial stability only by working a traditional job in which they are employed by someone else. This is simply not true and oftentimes keeps people from earning their full potential.

Second, some people think they want success, but in reality, they want to keep their life small and predictable. The idea of success is nice, but when pressed, many don't want to risk venturing outside of their comfort zone, making friends and family feel jealous, or having to file more complex tax returns. They are conditioned to accept whatever life gives them… and then complain about it.

I'm not here to tell you that shifting patterns is necessarily easy. But I can tell you it *is* possible. And that when you do so, it's the most inspiring and empowering experience you can have. You get to choose your intentions rather than just carrying out whatever reactive patterns are handed to you—the karmic package you don't want.

Shifting reactive patterns into your most desired intention takes effort, but it's the kind of effort that eventually becomes effortless, which is why it's so worthwhile.

Some families have very dark patterns to contend with—trauma, abuse, neglect, anger, or abandonment, just to name some. These terrible patterns can either keep repeating throughout the future, or they can be replaced with much more positive patterns, like commitment, dedication, determination, purpose, and inspiration.

The key to shifting patterns is to *act*. Additionally, we have to believe in what we're doing, and live in that new reality until we condition it into our experiences internally and externally.

My life's mission is to help people shift patterns that don't serve them. I've done this for decades as a psychologist and emotional scientist working with individuals and families, some of whom come to me with a debilitating mix of patterns. Some of these patterns destroy relationships and keep people stuck in cycles of depression, anxiety, substance abuse, attention deficit hyperactivity disorder (ADHD), autoimmune conditions, and other obstacles.

The crux of my work is to help people recognize their reactivity and then show them how to make a shift into intentionality. For instance, instead of a pattern of yelling at a spouse, we can collaborate on a new pattern of speaking calmly.

I've done this for countless clients, and my book can help you, too, shift dysfunctional patterns.

Before you bristle at the word *dysfunctional*, allow me to emphasize that everybody has negative patterns that hold them back. Do you know anyone who is perfect? I sure don't. Our patterns are part of what makes us human. The idea is not to pressure yourself to attain perfection, but rather to recognize patterns in your life. You get to decide which ones you want to keep. For patterns you want to shift, the tools here will help you make those changes.

That's why the chapters in this book include some of the most

Introduction

common patterns of humans in modern society. It's not just that *you* may struggle with something like reactivity—*most* people do. These chapters reveal patterns related to health, relationships, money, and purpose. They cover aspects of life that literally everyone will likely struggle with at some point or another.

The reality I choose to live in and shape is one in which everyone is gaining knowledge of intentionality. I've decided as well that this book will do that. It teaches you how to move from reactivity to intentionality, giving you an awareness of your life's patterns and how to shift any unwanted pattern from what it is to what you want.

A real change in your life is possible. The truth is anything is possible, and that's because of the creative mechanism. We are powerful creators, co-creating reality along with the Universe itself.

So give your life creative direction—your intention—because the mechanism is always *on*. Whether people acknowledge patterns or not, understand them or not, know how to navigate them or not, create the ones they intend or not, patterns are constantly occurring.

Introduction

In my intentional training company, we condition clients to select and replace patterns. Because people typically have a lot of patterns to identify, we do this conditioning over the course of a year. During those twelve months, various patterns of a person's life come up. This helps us see how these patterns manifest with their kids, parents, friends, and even strangers. And any of these patterns can be replaced—as many as the client wants. The person can create the reality they want, and it's an ongoing process that continues long after our work together is done.

The catch is that to truly and successfully replace a pattern, you need to be relentless about it. You need to totally and completely condition yourself for what you want. For example, rather than focusing on losing weight, you need to focus on what you are truly after—a healthy body that can help you achieve your goals. That becomes the focus, over and over. It becomes the reality that extends into everything, in every nook and cranny of your consciousness and existence.

It is much simpler than you might think. And having helped many, many people with this, I can attest that it works for absolutely anything and everything.

Now get ready to apply this intentionality to some of the most common patterns—and make the most powerful shifts that you can.

Understanding Patterns

Before getting into specifics, it's important to understand the reason patterns are so prevalent in human life. This foundational knowledge will help you learn why patterns keep coming up again and again—and how they impact not just us but the whole world.

Many daily patterns offer comfort and routine to our lives. But patterns are much more powerful than that. They rule everything in our existence—our minds and bodies, the earth, and reality. The natural world is chock-full of patterns we can witness going on all the time. The annual migration of birds north and south is a pattern; so is the thawing of winter into spring. Nature operates on its own, as if an unseen hand skillfully turns the leaves green in springtime, changes the weather, and directs the animals. For some people, this pattern-force is God, or Creation.

From an evolutionary perspective, humans are hardwired to identify patterns and create them. A study published in the scientific journal *Frontiers in Neuroscience*[2] states that our ability to recognize patterns—called superior pattern processing—is the basis of almost all features unique to the human brain. This includes our intelligence, language, imagination, invention, and even our belief in beings such as ghosts.

Essentially, patterns are what make us human. While animals follow patterns too, they aren't aware of them. But we are—and that's what makes us special.

As humans evolved, so did our ability to process patterns. The study emphasizes that patterns can be either real or imagined, and regardless of how valid they are, patterns are

---

[2] Mark P. Mattson, "Superior Pattern Processing is the Essence of the Evolved Human Brain," *Frontiers in Neuroscience* 8, no. 265 (August 2014), https://doi.org/10.3389/fnins.2014.00265.

reinforced by emotional experiences and social indoctrination. That means patterns are intricately linked to our emotions, and they become even more powerful when repeated by many people.

Science writer Dr. Michael Shermer[3] coined a term for our tendency to find meaningful patterns in meaningless chaos: *patternicity*. We create meaning from patterns we see—or just believe we see—in nature. This helps us with understanding our environment, with reproduction, and with our very survival.

Let's go back to the Stone Age. You hear rustling in a bush. Because you've seen other cave dwellers do so, you follow a pattern of running away as fast as you can. Now, it could be that this rustling was nothing more than the wind blowing. But it is also possible a dangerous animal was hiding in the bushes and getting ready to attack you. Following this pattern may have saved your life, and even if the noise was just wind, no harm came from your sprinting off.

---

[3] Michael Shermer, "Patternicity: Finding Meaningful Patterns in Meaningless Noise," *Scientific American*, December 1, 2008, https://www.scientific american.com/article/patternicity-finding-meaningful-patterns/.

Understanding Patterns

In modern times, often the patterns we see are real, but in some cases, they are just chance. These are referred to as *pattern recognition errors.* Think of hearing messages when a record is played backward, wild conspiracy theories, running from black cats, or seeing Jesus on a piece of toast. We love to ascribe meaning to things, even when we are in our imaginations.

But even beyond what we can see around us, patterns exist. Earth's orbit around the sun is a pattern. All of the planets rotate, along with the sun, in a counterclockwise pattern —except when they are briefly in retrograde, an opposite pattern.

It may seem like we are at the mercy of these unseen patterns, but that isn't the case. As we've seen in recent decades, humans' impact on the environment is altering the earth. Burning fossil fuels, deforestation of the Amazon, and other human actions have caused the earth's temperature to rise— and these patterns give way to other patterns that impact everything.

The dangerous western North America heat wave that affected parts of the United States and Canada in the summer of 2021 illustrates how one pattern can affect countless others. In a region where summer temperatures tend to be mild, the high reached 116 degrees Fahrenheit—the highest temperature ever recorded in the history of the area, which was simply not designed to function at that heat. The roads buckled due to thermal expansion, closing freeways. The heat distorted train rails and sparked wildfires. Fruit crops were lost on land, and in the ocean, millions of shellfish were literally cooked alive in the extreme water temperatures. Dead mussels appeared on the shore, split open from the heat.[4]

The unprecedented high was created by what climatologists call heat domes,[5] which are zones with strong, high pressure. This compresses air and heats it up, creating a pattern of hot, trapped air. A heat dome is made even more extreme by drought conditions since there isn't moisture in the ground to help cool the air. And the overall temperatures on Earth

---

[4] Shi En Kim, "Pacific Northwest and Canada's Crushing Heat Wave Cooks Millions of Sea Creatures," *Smithsonian Magazine*, July 12, 2021, https://www.smithsonianmag.com/smart-news/pacific-northwest-and-canadas-crushing-heat-wave-cooks-millions-sea-creatures-180978143/.

[5] Jason Samenow, Artur Galocha, and Diana Leonard, "The Science of Heat Domes and How Drought and Climate Change Make Them Worse," *The Washington Post*, July 10, 2021, https://www.washingtonpost.com/weather/2021/07/10/heat-dome-heat-wave-faq/.

are higher than ever, thanks to the burning of fossil fuels, so the temperature gets pushed up even more.

These patterns between the land and the atmosphere feed off of each other, creating a pattern of heat domes, which continue to scorch parts of the western United States.

Why am I giving you a science lesson? Man-made climate change demonstrates that we are not just at the mercy of nature. Really, *we* are forces of nature as well. While we may think our actions occur in a vacuum, they don't. We exist in an extensive matrix of patterns, although some people may willfully ignore them.

Just as patterns shape creation, patterns can be created. That means you are capable of shifting existing patterns and creating new ones—often in ways far more potent than you might realize.

Let's talk a little about the energy going on behind patterns. I love the word "emotion" because it's *e-motion*. We are always in motion, moving forward. If there's more emotion, there's more energy and intensity. And a lot of our patterns are related to emotions.

Even though we may feel separate from other people, we're not. We are all going forward together. And though we may feel apart from the world, we're gravitationally attached, so there's no separation. We are in constant cellular motion, and we get to decide what to do with that motion. That begets the following questions: What are you here to do? What are you bringing to this deal called life?

Handling stress poorly is a pattern, as is the pattern of being calm and steadfast. Your background gives you reference points of how you typically respond to stress, and when something has been going on so long in your history, it's got a lot of momentum if it's part of a longtime family dynamic. You are influenced by the way you were raised (nurture). But as discussed, genetics shape you as well (nature).

What I love about shifting patterns is that we have all this power of our actual DNA—the genetic building blocks that express how our body will work—and, just as important, we have the power of our emotional DNA, our karmic package. If your great-great-grandfather was born in Italy, it creates a reference point for you. That reference creates a reality—it's part of your identity. You might embrace this part of your identity by cooking Italian food, visiting the region in Italy where your grandfather lived, or learning to speak Italian. You don't have to do any of that, of course, but you would probably be more inclined than someone with no Italian heritage.

On the other hand, maybe your Italian background doesn't resonate very much with you. Your mother told you there's some Irish in your family, so you enjoy going all-out on St. Patrick's Day. Perhaps your spouse has family in France, and you find it a lot more fun to visit Paris with your kids and sip café au lait while eating a croissant—nothing wrong with that.

The good news is that with your identity you get to decide what you want to carry forward. You choose which parts you've inherited that you like or don't like. You can embrace and discard particular factors, even facets from the same parts of your identity.

Let's get back to the example of your family being partly Irish. You've gotten from your Emerald Isle ancestors a loyalty to family and faith, and you want to keep that sense of commitment. But then there are patterns such as self-medicating with alcohol because it was dark and cold in Ireland, and you don't want to carry that forward. This very powerful process of intentional training and reconditioning of patterns allows you to shift unsavory characteristics like brooding, moodiness, and self-medicating. You can decide instead to replace these patterns by drinking warm tea when it's dark and cold.

Making the PatternShifts

Patternshifts may initially seem more daunting than they actually are. While some are no doubt more difficult to change than others, you can condition yourself for something different, and then you get to choose. Instead of a behavior or response being handed down to you, like a set of patterns for depression, reactivity, or anger, you can take any of those and decide, *What would I like to replace this with?*

Even good patterns are replaceable. If you come from a family of people who are very enthusiastic and you're just not feeling it, you can replace enthusiasm with something like coolness. You get to decide what you want to experience.

Patterns are so powerful because whatever we focus on increases—it's just that simple. Thinking about what you *don't* want brings more of that unwanted element. If we say we don't want racism, we're still focusing on racism. But if we say we want equality, that shifts the pattern to what we really want. If all we are saying is that we want equality, we will do more of it. That's the reality of how patterns work.

We create our reality by giving it shape and doing it over and over, deciding which patterns we want in the world.

While there is an objective reality, that isn't where any of us live. In truth, everyone lives in their own reality. We each have our own perspective, not just because of our background and DNA, but because we are actively choosing our perception. We can choose what we focus on and what we're perceiving and amplify what we want. When you go outside, you can focus on how green the trees are, and they will look more vibrant as the leaves shimmer in the sun. Or you can downgrade them—if it's too bright, you can put on sunglasses while you observe the foliage.

We can also put our energy into another person to assess what their reality is and what they are feeling. When your child or pet is sick, you probably put all of your energy into identifying what's going on with them and how you can help them get better.

Understanding Patterns

Human beings are dialing their attention up or down all the time. They just don't quite understand how this actually works.

Whatever you want, the way to achieve it is to live that reality as if it's already here. You do that by conditioning it within yourself, not just outside of yourself. If you want to become a great tennis player, you not only buy a good racket and sign up for tennis lessons but also condition yourself mentally. You think about how fit you're getting, picture yourself winning on the court, and talk with others about your tennis matches.

When patterns pick up a lot of momentum, they can be hard to shift. As I mentioned, a lot of people are very focused on what they *don't* want. *I don't want to be stuck in this job. I don't want to have fish for dinner again.* But focusing on what you don't want keeps you stuck and feeling frustrated. You need to think about what you *do* want. This can take some practice when you're so used to thinking only in negative terms.

We see this with addictive patterns, too. Quitting smoking is so hard because, even if you mentally want to quit, you are physically addicted to nicotine. It's still possible to break this pattern, but it requires riding out the body's fierce protests during nicotine withdrawal—the pattern to which it's accustomed.

When you start to think about what you do want, you may then have a tendency to negate your desire. *Well, I'm not really sure. Maybe not right now. It's too much work.* But being in the energy of what you want shifts your physiology into a higher state. If you think, *I hate being fat*, you're still in the fat mindset. If you think, *I want to get more fit*, you perk up and flex your muscles. You are connected to that, and you activate more of that reality.

You first have to *feel* the shift, and then it can become a reality. When you say to yourself, *I want a husband and kids*, you feel the warmth of the family you're going to create. And when you consistently stay in that mindset, it becomes your reality.

Another example is when people think, *It takes a long time*, having been conditioned to believe certain achievements have to be really difficult to come by when they actually don't. Or maybe certain activities used to take a long time, but now with modern advances they don't need to, although some are still stuck in that old mentality. You might think, *This laundry is going to take all day*, when in reality, it should take very little time out of your routine with the use of modern washers and dryers.

Everything is being created through your thought patterns. If you get into a new relationship and tell the person, "I don't want to have my heart broken," you've set yourself up for a broken heart.

Anybody and everybody can build more emotional strength to make their intentions happen. Intentionality is the great equalizer that can help people bypass poverty patterns and whatever advantages other people have that they don't, like multigenerational wealth.

So while some people are in motion for poverty and others are in motion for wealth, it's possible to stop the motion, to shift these patterns. And it doesn't have to take a lifetime. You can basically do a cleanse of the old patterns, even those you were born into. Complexity can be replaced with efficiency, for example. It all depends on the degree of focus you are willing to place on your true desires. And if less desirable patterns are in play, you just shift them too.

Understanding Patterns

That's the reality of shifting patterns. You replace them and then live the new pattern you have chosen over and over again until it is as conditioned as the ones you did not choose and would probably never have chosen for yourself. You decide, *What is my next intention? What is my next outcome?* It takes you to the next moment, so you are creating new patterns rather than reacting to old ones.

Let's say the last time you spoke with your neighbor, you asked how his daughter was doing, but you forgot her name was Molly and called her Mindy. Since then, you haven't seen your neighbor outside. This pattern of absence convinces you that your neighbor is offended you forgot his daughter's name and is now avoiding you. Perhaps it also feeds into your long-standing fear of saying the wrong things to people, a pattern ingrained since childhood, when your mother corrected you in front of others for any little thing you said.

But without knowing for sure why you haven't seen your neighbor, your assumption may very well be an error. Maybe your neighbor is going through a very busy period at work. Maybe he's discovered a new hobby and is hanging out in his basement a lot. Maybe he thinks you're great, and he just has allergies this time of year, so he's been staying indoors.

Understanding Patterns

Rather than doubling down on your fearful pattern, you can decide that you simply don't know why you haven't seen your neighbor and that it's probably nothing to do with you. You might even shift this pattern by knocking on your neighbor's door to give him some vegetables from your garden and say hello to Molly (since your spouse reminded you of her name!).

So many of our patterns originate from times that predate us. While we may think we are evolved, we still grapple with old patterns, sometimes just in new ways.

Many people get nostalgic for the past. While we may miss the simplicity of eras gone by, many patterns, such as sexism or inequality, no longer serve us as a society. People may think they need to stay with those things rather than moving on, but that's actually the opposite of what we want to do as people.

We tend to stay with some patterns we are used to, even if they aren't serving us anymore. That's one of our characteristics as human beings. But this keeps us moving laterally or sometimes backward. But we are meant to move forward instead of living out, say, your grandfather's story of squalor and poverty. You get to have a brand-new moment with whatever you choose to focus on.

In that way, we are shifting the course of evolution. It doesn't matter what the pattern is—it could be rape, yelling, abuse, abandonment. It's easy to feel overwhelmed by life's problems—feeling we have to fix the government, the education system, the penal system, and a squeaky garage door. But if we talk about what we do want and focus on that, the whole dynamic changes.

That's what makes this process so amazing and yet so simple. Instead of going for depression treatment for twenty years, you can patternshift enthusiasm in place of depression, over and over, as you condition it. Certainly you should seek treatment for clinical depression if necessary, but the process doesn't need to be drawn out and difficult just because other people think it does. Instead of hanging out in depression, you can be in the emotional space you choose.

We exist in a world of patterns. When you acknowledge and accept this, your life gets easier—and it gets richer, as you notice patterns all around you. This alone is a level of awareness many people never achieve. Once you notice your patterns, you can take the next powerful step: shifting those you don't want in your life.

You may wonder what the replacement pattern should be for any given issue. Sometimes, it makes sense to choose the opposite. Instead of anger, choose calm or love. Instead of moving backward, move forward (in fact, that has its own chapter in this book!). But you can choose anything to be a replacement for a pattern you don't like. The only criteria is that the new pattern should make you feel like a better, stronger, happier version of yourself. If that means you replace eating ice cream with bird-watching, that's a great replacement.

With that said, let's dig into some of the most common patterns humans have that don't serve them—starting with being unconscious about their very lives.

PatternShift 1

UNCONSCIOUS TO CONSCIOUS

This first patternshift is the foundation for the others to come later, and that is moving from unconsciousness to consciousness.

This is incredibly important, because unconsciousness comes with a lot of suffering.

Unconsciousness is a state of being unaware of what's going on internally, and it can mean being unaware of what's happening externally, too. It's a whole experience that is ultimately lacking awareness, of being oblivious. It comes with a sense of confusion because you're not in alignment with the clarity that is meant for you.

PatternShift 1

You're not here to merely exist—you are engaged in a beautiful dance with the world, with reality, with God or the Universe. You can think of it simply as the earth's energy, if you aren't spiritual or religious. This higher consciousness is in communication with you all the time, constantly revealing itself to you. But you can't perceive it effectively if you are shut down—and most people are at least partially shut down.

To illustrate this, let me introduce you to the Taylor family. This isn't a real family but a composite of many real clients I've worked with over the years. The Taylors are a married couple—Linda and Jack—and they have two school-age children, Milo and Margot. In many ways, they are a typical American family.

But beyond their demographics, the Taylors are also a typical family in that they have deeply ingrained patterns that they act out every day with one another. Linda often struggles with anxiety and has chronic muscle tension. After the kids go to bed, Jack uses marijuana to numb his depression and the fallout from his traumatic childhood that he allows to still affect him decades later. When everyone is home, Milo and Margot are sometimes plunked in front of the

TV because their parents are too exhausted to engage in any family activities. As a result, the kids feel removed from their parents, even though they absorb Linda's and Jack's anxiety and depression just by being around it.

Linda and Jack both know they could do more to deal with their emotions and be fully present with their children, but it's tough. They both work, and life moves along quickly, even if they are often not very enthusiastic about it. The Taylors are a classic case of unconsciousness. They feel they are doing their best, but that's because they have internalized the idea that "life is hard" without challenging its patterns. It's causing the whole family to live short of their potential.

So unconsciousness is oblivion to what's really going on with yourself beneath the surface. But as you've probably seen, many people don't want to know what lurks in their psyches. How many times have you heard someone say, "Don't tell me. I don't even want to know!" While this statement can be a good-natured joke, in the big picture, we do not benefit from actively turning away from internal issues. Unconsciousness can cause suffering because it puts up a blind spot that blocks your view of life's fullness.

Unconsciousness is a major pattern in humanity. It's experiencing life as if it were happening *to* you, as if you were a passenger and not a copilot. You basically get beat up by life, thrown around by unseen forces because you aren't actively engaged with it. You're missing out on your full sensory capacity, and in fact, your full sense of the Self, which is your deepest, most in-tune nature.

With unconsciousness, life can feel very uncertain and full of negative surprises. You feel you have a heavy burden to carry, and your general disposition might be very flat at times. You're getting some drops of life, but wouldn't you rather drink up every single glorious bit raining down on you?

The Taylors are just trying to get by, so they go to work, pay their bills, shop for groceries, and make sure the kids get to school. But Linda and Jack always feel an underlying tension, a fear that something is going to go wrong, especially when it comes to finances. They worry that their car will break down and they won't have money for repairs, or that someone will get sick and the medical bills will pile up.

Some people get a sense that life is too big and overwhelming. They fall into a pattern of thinking life is a negative experience for them, so they shut life off, making the situation even more stressful. But you don't have to be bracing yourself all the time for life's hard knocks or putting in so much effort to barely get by.

Even if you try, you cannot ever truly be unconscious, despite your best efforts to tune out your surroundings. Think about it—even when you're asleep, you're alive. Your body is humming along, restoring energy, digesting food, and changing hormone levels.[6] This consciousness is running you, refreshing and preparing you for the coming day. Since you know your body is capable of doing so much on its own, think of how much you can do when you are awake and fully conscious! Consciousness *is* life.

Therefore, the replacement pattern for unconsciousness is consciousness. You consciously acknowledge that you are fully alive, that you are one with life. Consciousness is being who you really are, allowing life to create through you. That's because you create alongside Creation.

---

[6] Eric Suni and Ealena Callender, "What Happens When You Sleep?" *Sleep Foundation*, last modified August 11, 2022, https://www.sleepfoundation.org/how-sleep-works/what-happens-when-you-sleep.

When you make this shift, a state of unawareness is replaced with awareness—not of only the external world but also of your internal Self. I go much more in-depth about the inner Self in my previous book, *The Commitments: A Step-by-Step Guide to Personal Transformation*. For our purposes here, know that your inner Self is your internal navigation system. It's the voice that is able to remove itself from a situation and guide you based on your deepest values. Your inner Self tells you whether or not you're in a good relationship, what you need to be happy, and what you truly want.

Consciousness is about viscerally knowing you're alive. You don't need to be "on" all the time, but it's about striving to be in constant awareness.

If moving into consciousness seems daunting, remember that it's about following a pattern of awareness. This allows life to unfold for you. Awareness allows you to receive what you desire here on Earth. It's a state of both occurring and receiving, which also brings wisdom. It's a deep sense of peace, knowing the answers are within. It's the ultimate gift of life, to work in tandem with Creation.

Creation reaches out to all facets of life. This is about

consciously creating people, creating food, and creating ideas, just for starters. When you make this shift, your consciousness is in alignment with the life force. You are awake to the absolute, undeniable presence of what is occurring—its awesomeness and its simplicity. Consciousness is a liveliness that doesn't tire but rather encompasses *everything* you need or want or love. Consciousness points you the direction required for you to mindfully move forward in life.

Rather than feeling like she's a failure because her muscle tension is wearing her down, Linda can shift into awareness about why she is experiencing the physical discomfort. By being objectively aware, she recognizes her muscles are especially tense when talking to her boss or when she's rushing her kids from one overscheduled event to the next.

This awareness process gives you information about what is occurring and provides direction toward a solution. Purpose can now move through you, bringing with it a feeling of fullness, abundance, and the richness of life.

Moving into consciousness puts you in a position to be the receiver of life who you truly are. If you've given birth to a child, you've experienced the wonder of this process. During pregnancy, you receive life, and then you nurture this life inside of you as it grows. But even when not bearing a child, you are always a vessel for life, and life gets to make more of itself through you.

Although it may seem like consciousness would make difficult emotions worse, the opposite is true. At least for me, in this state, the questions fall away while the answers rise to the top. I feel the safety and security of being one with life. I feel deeply connected and taken care of and in my intended state of being.

That's because the consciousness that created us is the same consciousness that wants to keep creating us. It continually creates us, and awareness of that consciousness and its guidance is very important. It's the foundation of creating your best when you learn how to align with it.

When Linda applies her consciousness more fully, she becomes aware that her anxiety is not a problem to be fixed so much as her internal navigation system talking to her in a negative loop. It's telling her that her boss does not respect her. And it's telling her that keeping her kids busy with a lot of activities isn't helping them, because it's just creating more stress than enjoyment for the family.

Awareness includes us and the atmosphere. A lot of people are fearful that being aware means they will be shown aspects of themselves they don't want to see or will have to relive negative experiences. However, consciousness makes you aware of *all* aspects of your reality and can quickly help you see the positive aspects, too. Consciousness gives you a far more balanced picture of the world than when you're in a closed-off, unconscious state, fearful of what's happening or what you suspect might happen in the future. Consciousness is the pathway to integrity with your authentic Self and the world.

If you aren't sure how to implement consistent consciousness in your everyday life, don't worry. We all slip into unconsciousness sometimes. The key is to keep coming back to the present moment—not just placing awareness on what is happening around you but also on any thoughts, emotions, or sensations you are feeling inside. From there, you can check in with your intention for how to move forward. Then, keep coming back to that intention over and over.

Consciousness is truly a divine gift. And guess what—yes, you can handle it. In fact, you were born to be in this state, and it will carry on. When you die and leave your physical body, consciousness is the very essence of you that is still present. Of course, various religions and philosophies have different ideas, but even doctors suggest that consciousness survives after death.[7]

To me, that's a very glorious thing to experience, and it's a very empowering existence to live in.

Consciousness is about receiving quality of life versus rejecting or resisting the suffering. It's a process that is always in motion to transform life into its next best iteration. Consciousness is at the core of evolution, and unconsciousness is choosing to turn away from the natural evolutionary process.

So consciousness is always happening, 24/7. It is you. If your perception is on the other side, rejecting that you're part of this matrix, it doesn't change the fact that you are a player in it.

Sometimes, consciousness seems to get hijacked, despite our best efforts. If this is the case, going back to a pattern

---

[7] Kastalia Medrano, "Where Do You Go When You Die? The Increasing Signs That Human Consciousness Remains After Death," *Newsweek*, February 10, 2018, https://www.newsweek.com/where-do-you-go-when-you-die-increasing-signs-human-consciousness-after-death-800443.

of awareness is even more important. As an example, let's say Linda wakes up one morning and intends to go down to the kitchen and make breakfast for the family. She has twenty minutes before she has to get the kids up and ready for school so she can be at her office in time for a morning meeting.

As she scrambles eggs and fixes oatmeal, Jack comes into the kitchen. He starts talking about a list of household chores that need to happen over the course of the week. Linda shifts into a pattern of defensiveness. They argue about who is going to do what, who is busier, and how one doesn't appreciate anything the other does. Before it hits her, the kids are downstairs and breakfast isn't ready. Now Linda is stressed, even more pressed for time, and her kids will have to eat an energy bar on the way to school. She's shifted into another familiar pattern, feeling overwhelmed.

Linda didn't intentionally shift from her morning pattern into the defensive pattern, but with awareness, it would have been possible to tell Jack, "I hear you, and I want to discuss this with you. Let's talk tonight when we have more time." Because neither of them would feel pressure to hash out their chores before going to work, they wouldn't fight.

Believe it or not, unconsciousness is a choice. It's a program that is running along a track, and unless you retrain it, it will keep chugging along. Consciousness allows such a state of awareness that all of your intentions flow through any given experience so you are now running on a different program. Not only do you become more productive, but it also feels better. It's far more energizing to keep what you value at the forefront of your life than trying to outrun obstacles like a character in a video game.

Consciousness is deliberately taking the driver's seat and directing your intentions for the ride of your life. It feels natural because it *is*. We're meant to flow with life, not against it. Consciousness helps us follow a divine purpose not just in the grand scheme of existence but in your moment-to-moment reality.

Rather than stewing in a false belief that something is missing or lacking, direct your consciousness to create a full experience right here, right now. Tune in to your awareness, and get to know your true Self. You may be amazed by what you discover.

PatternShift 2

DISCONNECTED TO CONNECTED

Shifting from feeling disconnected to connected intimately correlates with the first patternshift of going from unconscious to conscious. They fit together, almost in a hologram.

Disconnection is a perceived separation from the Self, from others, and from life. It's a feeling of being unplugged, but not in the sense of relaxing or recharging. Because in actuality, we don't want to be unplugged from life. We want to be continually connected and intentional about what we do in that connection.

We have the ability to consciously connect to many things—another person during a conversation, a movie we're watching, or to ourselves in any number of situations.

Let's go back to the Taylors from the previous chapter. Linda and her husband, Jack, spend a fair amount of time being disconnected from their own Selves and from each other. They are also sometimes disconnected from Milo and Margot, their children. They go through the necessary steps to take care of the kids, but the demands of everyday life mean they are not always cognizant of how they act around them or why the kids act a certain way.

That isn't to say it's all gloom and doom. Many times Linda and Jack do feel connected. When grandma watches the kids and they go out together for a walk, they feel connected and have easy, truthful conversations. When the kids say funny things and everyone laughs, the whole family feels connected. When it's quiet and they each have time alone, they might spend a few minutes connecting to their reflections of the day. But their default pattern, which is deeply ingrained, is to be in disconnection.

When you feel disconnected, that perceived disconnection

creates more of itself. And when you aren't consciously connected to your surroundings, daily activities feel like they require more effort. You might feel alone, again not factual. Nearly eight billion people are on the earth,[8] so an almost infinite number of human lives are unfolding at once. And you, just like everyone else, have an almost infinite number of possibilities and experiences available to you.

Disconnection tends to come with more of a feeling of scarcity, too. How many times have you heard that there isn't enough in life—not enough food, not enough money, not enough resources, or not enough love to go around? Of course, focusing on lack creates the perception of more of lack as well.

As discussed, the mechanism of life is always *on*. But disconnection makes you feel like you might be stuck in a rut, when factually that's never true. You are never stuck because you have the ability to shift into something else. Every day you get up and are active, and then at night you shift into

---

[8] United Nations Population Fund, "World Population Dashboard," accessed August 29, 2022, https://www.unfpa.org/data/world-population-dashboard.

bed to go to sleep, but the process of your being a person is still running.

Without meaning to, people can feel they are on the outside of existence, instead of realizing the truth—that we're all insiders to the experience of life. Unlike being in the flow that allows life to be lived through us, feeling disconnected is hard work. So disconnection comes with all kinds of problems.

The biggest problem, of course, is being disconnected from yourself. You might try to get a feeling of connection from other people, and this has a dependent quality. While we're all here to collaborate, a high degree of self-containment is also necessary.

Both Taylors carry around a fair amount of frustration projected toward each other, and it's built up over the years. Jack tries to numb his most difficult feelings with marijuana use, but he also unloads some of his hurt onto Linda when at his lowest points. She then pulls away from him physically and emotionally, further driving a wedge between them, as she resents him for not being a present partner. They are not collaborating but coexisting in such a way that they are unhealthily codependent and disappointing each other at the same time.

Think of the survival film *Cast Away*. Tom Hanks's character is stranded on a deserted island, where he desperately wants to be rescued and be in the presence of other people. But as he continues his solitary existence, the process of life goes on. As long as he can harvest coconuts and spear fish, he is connected to life and able to survive. His character makes a shift, realizing he is connected to the life within him and around him, even in the absence of other humans.

Disconnection is also a pattern characterized by suffering and pain. My father passed away a few years ago, and as I write this, it's coming up on what would have been his birthday. Many people feel disconnected from the deceased, but I don't believe in disconnection. I'm actually more connected to my father now than when he was alive in physicality. You, too, can choose to live in the flow of connection.

Connection not only feels better but is also the reality. We are putting connection in its rightful place so we are one with ourselves, with life, with one another, and with the Universe. This is how we connect to the consciousness that has created us. We connect to ourselves as a vehicle for consciousness and to all of the wisdom that is being revealed to us.

The more connection is conditioned, the relationship with Self becomes what you intend it to be. You get to a point at which you have a connected relationship with yourself and your ability to observe, be intentional, and navigate the guidance offered you. All effort fades away, replaced with a flow state, which I refer to as an elevated state of consciousness.

Back to Linda and Jack—when they decide they are going to work on being better connected to their Selves, they each secretly worry they might realize they aren't meant to be together. After all, isn't that what usually happens when someone decides to "find themselves?" But actually, this process helps them become stronger as a couple.

When Jack spends more time listening to his inner Self, he recognizes how not dealing with his childhood issues causes his pendulum to swing from closing down to lashing out. He stops projecting his frustrations onto Linda, who in turn sees that her shutting Jack out contributed to their rifts as well. They are in tune with themselves, so they can be in tune with each other—and with much less effort than before.

Connection is where everything is available and life feels so good. Food tastes amazing, what you do feels incredible, life feels rich, and you get the best out of every experience. It's the quality of receiving whatever is brought forth in any moment. Connection is where the barriers go away and the sense of separation shifts into a beautiful, intentional flow, which we'll see even more of as we move into other patternshifts.

Many people are conditioned to view life with a sense of limits. *Some people have everything, while others have nothing, and that's just how life is.* But when you tap into connection instead of perceiving that some people receive the bulk of life's blessings while others are left in the dark, you realize a very different quality of existence in which no one is missing out on anything. Nobody is confused about what's next and how to follow their intentions.

If you're being prompted for nourishment, you move in the direction of eating. If you're being prompted to feel affection, you pet your dog. And if you're being prompted to tell a deeper truth to someone, you go with that. Connection is alignment with yourself and with life, and why you're here.

It's like being in partnership with Self, with enough awareness to check yourself and keep yourself in your own lane, even if you are closely picking up on the energy of someone who is in a confused pattern. You so deeply connect to yourself that you continue on your trusted path rather than letting someone else's confusion stop you in your tracks.

If you plunk down on the couch at the end of the day to watch Netflix, you may think, *Oh, I'm stopping*, or, *I'm taking a break*. Well, not really. Nobody's actually stopping life. But what you are doing is deciding whatever you want next. You can decide to watch a show you like, you can choose to get on your phone to text with a friend, or you might opt to look out the window to appreciate the setting sun's rays shining through the trees.

When Jack feels more connected, he catches himself when he disengages and feels the urge to smoke marijuana. Instead of opting to light up, he thinks more about what he wants to be connected to next. He may decide he wants to talk to Linda about a work situation. As they talk, he feels increasingly close to her, and she to him. From there, they can co-create together, and they make plans to take the kids to the beach for the weekend for some family fun.

Connection is that state in which you get to receive everything on your personal wish list. It's the whole process that's supposed to be going on, versus the inaccurate patterns holding us back. These are a confusion of beliefs due to conditioning. We are meant to be connected to the safety and security of our true Self and what that state of being allows us to do.

I'm a passionate ballroom dancer. When I'm training for a dance, I spend ninety minutes to two hours practicing at least five times a week. The quality of what I'm doing is about being connected to all parts of myself. I'm not just connected to my individual body parts such as my feet, thighs, and arms—I'm connected to my Self and all the wisdom available to me.

As I go through that dance training process, whatever isn't authentic to my Self is removed from my emotional field, and I intentionally go deeper within my psyche. My connection leads to an expanded cellular consciousness, and then my body does what it is meant to do. My body parts work together to become the dance. It's a continuous system in which my knees are meant to work with my hips to take me through the dance steps.

Perhaps you, too, have felt this while participating in an activity or hobby you love. Your body is supporting and carrying you, but your deeper Self is propelling you through creative expression.

When you're not fully connected with your whole Self, it's as if only fragments of yourself are carrying out certain activities. It feels like way more effort than it should be, and that's because it is.

But when you are in connection to life force, and you get it and feel it intimately, that is also when you realize this is your natural state. This is where the effort is gone and you don't have to overthink anything.

When I dance, I don't have to think about the movement of every single part of my body. I don't have to think to get my hands and feet moving simultaneously. It's more about connecting to the energy field, which is happening all the time.

When I warm up to dance, I start by stretching. Then I bring myself into alignment, feeling my whole being. I recognize that it's just about staying there and being in that continuous connection. But then all of a sudden, my mind might wander. Perhaps I think about a client situation and what I want to bring to it. And it's the very thing that happens with humans.

We end up somewhere on another track and often don't even realize when we've veered off into unwanted territory.

But then I bring myself present, and I keep staying there—I stay there, stay there, stay there. Sometimes it takes a few seconds; other times it's two minutes, and then others longer. At times, several seconds later, I'm already off on another track. I think, *Okay, forward again*. I reconnect and say to myself, *Connect, connect, connect*.

If I were to say, *Oh, you're off track*, now I would be detouring even further. But when I tell myself to *connect*, I set myself up to stay longer in connection. And my intention remains to be one with the dance. The more you connect and remain in connection, the more it becomes your new conditioning—an elevated state.

Linda, of the fictional Taylor family, may have the intention to stay calm all day, but she will be pulled in many different directions as she tends to her children and co-creates with her husband. The effects of a newly established routine of morning meditation may quickly wear off as Milo and Margot fight over toys. When a toy gets flushed down the toilet, causing dubious burping sounds in the commode, Linda might teeter way off center. It's easy to see how anyone can suddenly get on a frazzled, reactive track.

But the more awareness you foster, the more you can acknowledge when you become disconnected or allow yourself to be pulled in a direction that is opposite your intention. Connection is the very important setup for even more intentionality.

This patternshift can feel challenging if you haven't felt much connection in the past to your desires. How can you have a happy family if you did not grow up with that model? Even if you don't have much firsthand experience with happy families, imagine the qualities you want your family to embody. *We laugh and have fun. We are organized. We talk calmly to one another.* Focus on these qualities, over and over, and you will get there.

The real challenge is to stay in that connection, to condition yourself to be in connection. Have fun with it! Choose to be more connected to your authenticity than to another person's expectations of you. Make a decision to be connected in joy. It's a foundational pattern because you get to add other things to it, which makes them all better with each other.

Whenever you perceive disconnection in yourself, completely replace that with connection in the present moment and intend it for the future, too. This patternshift leads to a major upgrade to your life. Just like when you get an upgrade on your phone, the operating system isn't going to go back to the old version.

Connection is tuning in to reality, embracing it, and co-creating with the Universe to manifest the future you want. Connection makes you unstoppable.

PatternShift 3

NEGATIVE TO POSITIVE

Almost everyone struggles at one point or another with shifting thoughts and words from negative to positive. The negative, simply put, is all about what *isn't*—what isn't happening, what isn't there, what somebody isn't doing, what you don't have. It's a pattern of emptiness and scarcity, and even though it's so pervasive, it's also highly delusional. Negativity has been ingrained in society going back millennia, and we've been conditioned to speak in familiar refrains about what seems off about any given situation. This can manifest in many familiar refrains: "Something's wrong." "There isn't enough." "The world sucks." "People are terrible." It's the dark view, the empty void. Negativity is meaningless and purposeless.

Even when expressed with good intentions, negativity isn't helpful. Jack might say to Linda, "I'm taking out the trash because I don't want you to have to do it." He's being thoughtful, but his statement still places a focus on what Linda *isn't* doing. A patternshift for this scenario might be that Jack says to his wife, "I'll take out the trash so you can find us a movie to watch." That simple change in wording turns the statement in the other direction to what *is* going to happen. The action of taking out the trash is moving the couple toward a positive moment, the ability to bond and spend time together.

This verbal shift may not seem like a big deal, but it is deceptively powerful. We are all here to live in a state of intention with the Universe. When you do that, you can't help but be positive—you are in tune with everything you're receiving, everything flowing through you, everything available to you, and everything that is stunning and beautiful.

You see, a negative reality doesn't only feel worse than a positive one. When you're in the negative, you live in an inconsistent reality—one that is sometimes in the positive and sometimes in the negative. That relentless back-and-forth is destabilizing, and it's not accurate. A negative reality can also lead to the worst possible outcomes, because that negativity creates more of itself as long as you are giving it attention.

In dog training, the trainers have shifted from negative to positive reinforcement over the years. Training used to be about what a dog *shouldn't* do: "Don't get on the couch." "Don't pee on the floor." Now, when a dog potties where it's supposed to, the trainer reinforces that good behavior because it's what the dog *should* do: "Good dog! You peed outside in your spot." The dog will exhibit more of that positive behavior in response to the positive reinforcement.

Well, training ourselves for positivity isn't much different. And one of the best parts of it is that positivity becomes a lot easier and more fun with every pleasant interaction. Your positivity expands with every conversation you have about what you're intending, what you want, what you're excited about, what is flowing, what is going well, what is working out, and what is improving.

Have you ever heard of the Pareto principle, also known as the 80/20 rule? It's a business theory that states 80 percent of our outcomes (outputs) result from 20 percent of all incomes (inputs).[9] In business, this can mean focusing on marketing to the 20 percent of clients who are responsible for 80 percent of the company's revenue. The 80/20 rule can be applied to any field, including psychology. How many people do you know who spend 80 percent of their time focused on the 20 percent of their life that isn't going well? On the flip side, if even just 20 percent of your life is going well and you keep your thoughts predominantly on those positive aspects, you can yield an 80 percent increase in your positivity, which dramatically improves your life.

I want to add a disclaimer about positivity. A lot of people see positivity as a delusion. Let me be clear that when I talk about shifting from negativity to positivity, I'm not suggesting that you ignore reality. Some experiences in life are objectively negative and painful. What I'm saying is to think about which experiences can best be shifted to the positive, because many of them can be.

---

[9] Kevin Kruse, "The 80/20 Rule and How It Can Change Your Life," *Forbes*, March 7, 2016, https://www.forbes.com/sites/kevinkruse/2016/03/07/80-20-rule.

Being in the negative the majority of your time destabilizes not just your mind but also your body and physical health. If your focus is on pain, suffering, and illness, more of these show up in your experience. Focusing on ailments is essentially discounting the way your body works and its ability to heal. It discounts the way the Earth works, and the Universe beyond. When you focus instead on the innate wisdom and abilities of the world, including your body's cellular knowledge, those positive aspects grow in you. Your consciousness of the positive and the affirmative expands also as you share your positive outlook with other people.

Anytime you say something positive to another person or speak to others about something joyful, you're conditioning them so they, too, feel the truth of a positive well-being. Positivity is contagious! It inspires other people to create positively, too, so it's a very powerful shift.

As parents, Jack and Linda have the opportunity to powerfully shape not only their own realities but their children's as well. Instead of dreading taking Milo and Margot to the dentist's office, they can talk to their kids about how the dentist keeps their teeth strong and healthy, and they can plan a fun activity to do after the appointment. While Milo and Margot may pick up from other people that going to the dentist is scary or stressful, their parents can shift this into a positive experience.

The negative feels horrible and stressful. As I write in my previous book, *The Commitments: A Step-by-Step Guide to Personal Transformation*, this can manifest in many ways, from addictions to anxiety and depression to broken relationships.

When Linda is stuck in the negative, life feels empty for her. She looks at a situation and thinks only about what is missing from her life. When she and Jack throw a party, she doesn't rejoice in the friends and family who are there to have a wonderful time—she focuses on the people who didn't show up. She's already planning her next party in her head and what she wants to do differently.

Although this patternshift may seem difficult, it's actually very simple. Anytime you describe something that *isn't*, catch yourself and realize you are creating a negative experience. It may seem like the only reality, but that isn't the case; it is only the negative reality, and some people live in it constantly. Instead of saying, "At least it isn't raining," you can say, "It's overcast and cool—good walking weather."

Maybe you know people who live in a seemingly never-ending state of negativity. They cling to the bottom rung of life, complaining nonstop, convinced the world is out to get them. They may say, "I don't want to be sick," but by talking about what they don't want, they are still conditioning their bodies to be sick. Then there are other people—most people, in my experience—who live in a split reality that vacillates between positive and negative. They have some good things going on in their lives, but they get derailed when circumstances change. Shifting into the positive can be entirely life-changing. "I don't want to be sick," or even "I want to be healthy," can turn into "I am healthy and living my best life in each moment."

Strive to be proactively positive with every single thing you think, feel, or say. Speak mindfully, with diligence and discipline to come to a point where you are conditioned for positivity. Your life is a reflection of how you're perceiving it, in its ease, beauty, and flow. You're seeing the fabulous future and thinking, *Life is so incredibly full, abundant, and magical, in the best practical way.*

A lot of people think negative thoughts but do not verbalize them. Maybe you were raised with the idea that *If you can't say anything nice, don't say anything at all.* But this shift goes not only for what you're verbalizing to the outside world but also your internal self-talk—your innermost thoughts. While it may sound daunting, your thoughts are quite powerful. What we create within ourselves changes the world.

This positivity means that every single thing you proactively condition yourself for or everything that is, you speak about it. You talk about what you want, what you're doing, what you intend, what you're liking, what is occurring, and what will be occurring. When something negative comes up, you can simply say, *No, thank you*, to this alternative.

A lot of our social interactions have conditioned us to turn complaining into a competitive sport. When Jack asks Linda about her workday, she talks about the one thing that didn't go well—a coworker cut her off when she had the floor during a meeting. She doesn't mention the laughs she enjoyed with another coworker over lunch or that she finished an important project ahead of a deadline. As Jack commiserates, he talks about the small trivialities from his day as well.

The positive side of life is waiting for you to notice it so it can expand in your experience. For those who doubt the magic of life in all its amazingness, let me remind you that this blue planet we inhabit is rotating around a star that's on fire and lighting everything up, and we have a moon that along with the sun is influencing the ocean's tides.[10] Remember to revel in the absolute beauty of which you are a valued part.

Jack and Linda pick up on this magic in subtle ways. When they take a family vacation to the beach, they stop to watch the beauty as the sun sets and bathes the ocean and sky in an array of colors. When Milo and Margot were each born, time stood still for Jack and Linda as they held their babies for the first time and felt the miracle of these new lives they had co-created.

This patternshift into an elevated state and this conditioning make it so that you live life in the reality where everything is beautifully available to you. It is perfectly arriving to you, and it is there for you to order up and pick out. And you're just delighted in it.

---

[10] Fraser Cain, "Earth, Sun and Moon," *Universe Today* (blog), March 12, 2009, https://www.universetoday.com/26987/earth-sun-and-moon/.

Let's say Linda, Jack, and the kids are going to Italy in June. As they anticipate their trip, they feel positive excitement, and they are in that reality. They talk to their friends and coworkers about the trip. They imagine all of the delicious meals they will eat and picture themselves enjoying gelato in a café. They research all the artwork they plan to take the kids to see.

All of this positivity and preparation makes it that much more likely they will have a wonderful experience when they go—even if some things don't go exactly as planned. The Universe stacks everything in their favor because they are powerful creators. And that reality is very potent, because like everyone, Linda and Jack are powerful creators.

Like the Taylors, you have free will. You have the ability to choose, so choose positivity. When you choose positivity, you live positively. If anybody ever says to you, "Oh, you're too upbeat and positive," take that as a compliment and amp it up!

You can respond by saying, "Exactly, and I am actually on my way to being even more positive." And you can just keep adding onto it.

Even though some people deny it, everyone wants positivity. How many people do you know who truly want to be miserable? Those who are unhappy are looking for a way out but may feel stuck and frustrated.

The funny thing is that the negative pattern gives the positive a bad reputation. Negativity says that positivity isn't realistic. But is it more realistic to be negative all the time? When you are in the positive, you're in the flow. That's where life is full and everything is available to you. That is a lot more realistic than being shut off from life's pleasures.

I invite you to primarily replace your negativity with positivity. It's an invitation that can touch every aspect of your life. You are invited into the experience of positivity and the entire world that is running, and you turn the lights on to it. This is now your reality, and you can fully embody it to enjoy all that is rightfully yours. Know that it is a beautiful, infinite, expansive experience that allows you to easily see the world and the Universe with clarity and appreciation in any moment, location, or scenario. It allows you to fully comprehend, love, and reside in this world.

Enjoy the upgrade, because it's where you get to live to your fullest potential. It's a beautiful place, and I'm happy to have you here with me.

PatternShift 4

REACTION TO INTENTION

So many people live in reaction, either part of the time or nearly all the time, and it can make them miserable.

How often do you react to life as opposed to intending? You may not be actively aware of this, but an easy way to figure it out is by gauging how much time you spend feeling tense or stressed (reaction) and time spent feeling relaxed or "in the zone" of what you're doing (intention). Simply put, being in reaction mode usually feels bad while being in intention feels good. So you want to shift from being in a reactive state to an intentional one, over and over, until intention is your default most of the time.

Let's take the same person having the same experience but living it in each possible scenario—intention and reaction. When Jack goes to the grocery store in an intentional state, he is there to buy food to nourish his family. He has his grocery list and gets through the store efficiently. In line waiting to purchase the food, he is calm and content, thinking about the next outcome he'll create after he leaves the store—perhaps the delicious dinner he and his wife will cook together with some of the fresh ingredients he's bought.

In contrast, this is what the pattern of reactivity does: Jack is in an unconscious, disconnected, negative pattern in which he responds to life in a reactive way rather than allowing life to flow through him based on his intentions. In this version of events, Jack feels irritated with other shoppers in the store. He forgets items on his list and then gets more frustrated as he has to go up and down aisles to look for them. He can't think of anything beyond his own annoyance.

Rather than life flowing through you in all of its expressions—in your physiology, your communication, and your conversation—reactivity is a pattern of resistance. It is the misperception that life is happening *to* you, and that's drudgery. It feels overwhelming. Reactivity has this quality by which nearly everything seems to be about suffering and pain with only small pockets of relief or enjoyment. Even describing it here, I feel tension and resistance build in my body.

Reactivity is fearful, as if you have no control over what's happening. It's a resistance of life, and it's been conditioned into a surprising number of us. Reaction is repeating stories about life being bad, and every time a situation seems less than ideal, it gets filed away as negative, which reinforces it even more. So reactivity can essentially be a mashup of the unconscious, the disconnected, and the negative.

Obviously, consistently living in reactivity isn't good for anyone. But reactivity can tell a captivating story, often reinforced by society. How many reality shows spotlight people who are in a deeply reactive state as a way of entertaining television audiences? Whether manufactured or real, these shows take one person's innocuous statement and turn it into a fight with another. Yelling, table-flipping, and storming out of the room may ensue. Even if we don't believe in its authenticity, the narrative of reaction keeps many viewers spellbound. Watching other people behave badly lets others live vicariously in reactivity, even for those who wouldn't act out to that extreme in their own lives.

But any form of reactivity you're exposed to has an effect on you. Reactivity, like other patterns, is a chain of energy that can keep running, making more of itself. I think of reactivity being more like *radioactivity*. It's like life is a ticking time bomb about to go off. But none of this is true—it's what's been programmed into your consciousness. In fact, reactivity is often just reality misinterpreted.

When Linda is in a reactive state, she may be harder on her kids than she normally would be. She may accuse Milo and Margot of taking dessert out of the freezer before dinner, only to later remember *she* took a clandestine bite of the ice cream and then forgot to put it back. Then she feels bad for being short with the kids.

Reactivity can be painful, so it would behoove you to replace it with intentionality. Let me be clear about what that entails: I don't mean briefly thinking about your dream life and then sliding right back into a complaining, reactive mindset. Intention is a permanent state, a glamorous, luxurious, elevated state in which you're one with life. You and life are co-creating ever-evolving *you*.

Life created you. You *are* life. All of life is running you, your whole system. The replacement for this pattern is that instead of being in the reactive programming you're currently in, you consciously tap into intention. You're an integral part of life as an entire operating system, so intentionality is everything that is flowing through you, even in the midst of reactivity of others in the world.

This is how we are meant to operate. Intentionality utilizes you as a vehicle of evolution. Life flows through you, moving your body and activating you. The key is to be in alignment with it as it's going instead of lagging behind it. Intentionality asks you to steer it in the direction of what you want, so we are all co-creating a shared life together.

A lot of Jack's reactivity comes from the fact that he doesn't like his job. He's been employed there for years and makes good money, so he believes he has to keep showing up every day in order to support his family. Then Jack thinks more about the fact that he feels most intentional at work when he mentors younger colleagues. Tapping into this flow, he decides to start a side gig as a business coach. He becomes increasingly excited as he builds his business, and then he decides to take the leap into full-time business coaching.

This intentionality is the receiving of everything. Everything is available to you—the whole world is yours. All of the material in it, its whole reality, is yours. And you belong to it as well. This experience of intentionality is the elevated realm of existence where everyone is meant to reside. It's not meant to be a short-term visit. Unpack your bags and settle in, knowing this is a permanent staycation.

Despite whatever is going viral or trending, the sun will rise and set. All of life's natural cycles will keep going, and being in intentionality means being in sync with these cycles. Instead of hanging on to the latest distractions, you are deeply and fully connected to the joyful flow of life.

So where reactivity is the resistance, intentionality is the allowing, the expression, and the expansion of life that wants to be expressed and not suppressed. It wants acceptance and nonresistance. It says simply, *Come along, come forward, come give the direction—shape it, decorate it, design it, beautify it, and give it your unique touch.*

As human beings, we are evolving the world. That's how powerful we are. This pattern is one in which we condition all that we intend. So you might ask yourself, *What is my intention?*

Programming yourself for your intentions is not as difficult as you may assume. You've programmed yourself, without much effort, to brush your teeth, to shower, and to drink water. You barely, if at all, have to think about lifting your hand to hold up a pen. When you first learned to use a pen, it was awkward to hold. You may have dropped it and gotten frustrated as you tried to write with it. But now when you pick up a pen, it's life moving through you. Life is flowing instead of your having to struggle with it. This is about conditioning intentionality so thoroughly that nothing else exists. And if something else pops into your field of awareness, you immediately convert to intentionality.

The strange thing about reactivity is that it causes you to wrangle and fight, even though it's a passive state. In contrast, intentionality is an active state. Instead of deciding that a situation is going to be horrible, you choose to believe that it will bring a good outcome, that everyone will be smiling.

This is your imagination, but it's also your life's purpose flowing through you. When she is deliberately directing her intentionality, Linda finds that even a mundane task such as taking the kids to the playground takes on a magical dimension. She thinks ahead about how the park is so green, the beautiful drive to get there, and the incredible clouds and blue skies overhead. She sees the park through the kids' eyes—how fun it is to be there.

Whatever it is you came here to contribute, you came here to create with ease by standing in the power of your intention. You are meant to be in intention all the time so that just like driving a car, it becomes second nature. Then it goes into your subconscious, allowing the receiving, the expanding, and the expressing of intentionality to roll through. Your past reactive behavior becomes no more than a fleeting speck of history.

You could categorize all of the world's problems as products of reactivity. All problems shift to their solutions when you make intentionality your priority and exist in the elevated state you were born to be in. And we transform ourselves into that sense so that there is nothing else occurring: this is our great purpose.

When you find yourself reacting to something, you may wonder what sort of intention you should replace it with. That's the fun part—you can replace it with anything you want! You can replace frustration with inspiration, for example, or frustration with expansion. When Jack feels bored, he can decide to replace boredom with the freedom to try a new activity. Or he can replace boredom with excitement about the task he's doing. The possibilities are endless.

When you consciously apply positive intention, in every single experience and conversation and interaction, you are the living, breathing, conscious, connected, positive, productive, creative force of nature. You leave behind the old pattern, which you never really wanted in the first place.

In any moment where you drop out of consciousness and your full creative capacity, you get alerted with a little jolt of pain or discomfort. This is normal, so don't get sidetracked by a small blip in the radar. You simply resume forward into your intentions and flip that switch.

As you trust your intentions, they make more of themselves. They become a chain of intentions that shape your world. You fill in your reality with all of the details you intend rather than having some other version in which reactivity gets to run the show. When you stay in a state of intention, you are the master director.

Whatever you want, whatever you intend, whatever you wish becomes conditioned because intentionality is always available. It is inviting you to become one with it. This is why in every way, every day, every moment you speak the language of intentions to yourself—you *feel* your intentions. You reveal them and communicate them as you interact with other people.

If someone wants a different intention than yours, you can simply think, *What is it that I want? What do I intend?* Then make the internal shift so it's in the atmosphere. You may very well find that the other person says or does what you intended—that's how powerful intentionality is. Or the Universe might deliver the perfect solution that combines the wanted elements of the other person's intention with yours.

Take the example of climate change. Many of us are intending to reverse the climate crisis so our planet is healthier, especially for future generations. We can intend that clean air replaces dirty air. So we talk about clean air in our conversations: "We're so excited to have clean air—it's so amazing." "We're going to have clean air for the rest of our life." "We're here to have clean air and make the air clean."

We also clean the air with our intentionality. Every single intention makes our environment clean, and every single reaction makes it dirty. Since we want to clean the air, we speak it, and live it. We follow this intention on every physical and metaphysical level.

I'm inviting you to fully replace reactions with intentions. You run into your neighbor, your friend calls, you send a text, you are on a project with a client—with anyone you're speaking to, choose to say, "This is what is so exciting. This is what's going well. This is what's improving." That's how you live your positive intentions and keep building more of them.

Linda loves Jack, but she often wishes he were more ambitious. She intends for this to happen, and while she doesn't pressure him, she helps him embody the essence of ambition. Linda encourages him to take healthy risks in his career, and her enthusiasm boosts his confidence and allows the upgrade to become a reality.

With whom are we co-creating reality? Whether you think of it as Life, God, the Universe, or the Creator, co-creation is always happening. He, She, or It is always listening and communicating with us.

All of us at some point feel we have intended for something to happen and it didn't. The thing is, because it is a co-creative process, life can unfold as a multifaceted experience that is even more dimensional than you intended. And that is because *we* are multidimensional, creating with all of ourselves from every cell of our beings in the environment. But if you are steady in your intentions, keeping them positive and staying open to the feedback you are getting from universal energy, your intention has to eventually become a reality.

A client was explaining to me some outcomes of directing his intentions. He talked about how he shifted so that he felt a more intentional emotion instead of a reactive emotion. Referring to his shifting emotions, he said, "But I don't know if that's a practical outcome, a practical result." I had a hearty laugh, because it's *the* most practical result. Although they may not seem like it, practical and emotional are the same thing. When you tap into your true emotions, they will lead you where you need to go.

Emotional evolution makes everything happen. Being consciously intentional can be exhilarating and relaxing at the same time. We each get to make a beautiful, amazing order to the Universe: beauty? Love? Time? Joy? What's on your checklist? What is the unique package you are creating? Intentions are fabulous because you get to choose what you want and then let the Universe make a special delivery to you.

PatternShift 5

BACKWARD TO FORWARD

Let's delve into another common pattern tied to resistance: the pattern of moving backward. This is problematic because, as discussed, life is always in forward motion. It's the simple physics of our reality—the earth moves forward. And if you go in reverse, you're going in the opposite direction of life.

You're probably familiar with what it feels like to move backward. When you ruminate on what happened in the past—how you should have handled a situation, how something was so stressful, how much someone hurt you—it's not a pleasant feeling. Even thinking back on good memories can sometimes bring heartache, perhaps a feeling of longing for the way that things used to be.

When you go backward, you're out of touch with the present moment, and the future you're creating is also out of focus. We know evolution and forward movement are occurring—that is a fact of existence. Going backward is reverting attention to a previous experience, which of course we can't even fully do because we are no longer in that moment. Going backward takes a lot of attention and focus, because it means you're swimming against the current.

That attention and focus are best directed to the here and now, to what you are actually receiving in the moment—which carries you forward.

When you are in your body and in tune with your Self, you are consciously here in this moment, going forward and connecting to your intention and the navigation that is coming in, flowing through you. When you're focusing on a backward pattern, your mind is elsewhere, reliving, redoing, rehashing, and re-experiencing—and possibly resenting, too. While many memories are pleasant, some are associated with pain.

We are given free will to choose to live either in a backward or forward pattern, and intentionally creating forward allows life to flow through us.

When Jack and Linda feel stressed about their kids, they sometimes think back to the time in their relationship before Milo and Margot were born. They get nostalgic for memories of sleeping in, long brunches with friends, spontaneous outings, and plenty of alone time. But going backward doesn't offer them much in the present moment, and it doesn't help them move forward, either. It just makes them less present with their children, and all the time they spend thinking of how things used to be—or how they choose to remember it—could be spent thinking of the ideal future they want to have as a family.

How do you shift from moving backward into forward momentum? The clearest path is to speak only of the future reality you are choosing. That reality is being constructed and created because you are thinking it, feeling it, speaking it, and acting it into being with every single reference point of anything you want.

Instead of thinking about their prechild days, Jack and Linda can plan and talk about what they want to do in the coming months—they might build a swing in the backyard or arrange a visit with the grandparents. Knowing their children's varying interests, they can have a family outing to a petting farm since Milo loves horses, and they can also go to a basketball game since Margot loves the sport. There are countless options, and the Taylors are now moving forward together in a shared vision of the family.

One reason backward needs to be replaced with forward is because it is so disorienting. The future is our true orientation—both being in the now and looking toward the future. The now, in fact, *is* the future, and the future is the now that you are creating. Going backward is nothing but a conditioned emotional pattern; it's not your current reality.

Think about it—the patterns that hold you back were all created in the past, and you keep reliving them over and over. These patterns may have been forged generations ago in your family. They are kept alive through false conditioning that says you have to keep holding on to them, that they are your inheritance.

When Jack gets upset, he has a tendency to yell. His outbursts are short-lived, but this is a common reaction when he feels stressed. He doesn't necessarily like doing it, but he also doesn't think much about it because it was conditioned into him by his father, who yelled when things didn't go his way. This is Jack's reference point for how to react to unpleasant occurrences. When Linda says she doesn't like his yelling, Jack shrugs it off. "That's just the way I am," he says.

But this isn't really true. This is the way Jack *chooses* to be. He chooses to relive and repeat his father's reactions, even though he didn't like it when he was a child. He has taken on this conditioning as his perceived reality, and by extension, made it seem real for his wife and children.

We've always had power to create reality, to co-create with everything and everyone in the Universe. We also have the ability to go backward and extract something we might want to take forward with us—that is a privilege and a choice, to choose where we are going to be in any given moment.

As with anything you concentrate on, when you go into the past, it creates more of itself, which is really fascinating. The more you connect with your personal history, the more you live it and relive it. We continue to live a collective past in a society as well in many ways. We re-experience the same things over and over until we've gained some knowledge to shift to healthier, forward-moving patterns.

The fundamental shift that needs to happen is that the knowledge we learn as a society *is only applied forward.* Otherwise, if human knowledge continues to focus the past into reality, it keeps perpetuating the unpleasant, unproductive, and destructive patterns in humanity.

Albert Einstein is attributed as saying, "We cannot solve our problems with the same thinking we used when we created them."[11] A lot of businesses have failed because they made the mistake of being mired in past thinking. Rather than focus on innovation and changing with the times, some businesses stick to what made them successful in the past, but sometimes that is not enough.

The Kodak camera company is an example of this. Once the leader in photography, the company didn't capitalize

---

[11] David Mielach, "'We Can't Solve Problems By Using the Same Kind of Thinking We Used When We Created Them,'" Business News Daily, *Business Insider*, April 19, 2012, https://www.businessinsider.com/we-cant-solve-problems-by-using-the-same-kind-of-thinking-we-used-when-we-created-them-2012-4.

on the digital camera movement, because it didn't want to disrupt its film roll business. As other companies got better and better at manufacturing and marketing digital cameras, Kodak was left behind in the past it was trying to recreate. The company filed for bankruptcy in 2012.[12]

What you focus on in the present, what you condition, and how you condition it—those are what you carry forward. So make sure you are creating where and what you intend. Selecting and conditioning what you intend are key. Because the conditioning makes more of itself, we keep creating only what we want, going forward with ease. That is the biggest, most massive upgrade of this patternshift.

Humans are really something: we have the ability to focus, connect experiences, be conditioned, and train and elevate our minds, so we can take ourselves anywhere in any experience. When you explore life, you are given the keys to the kingdom. You get to choose where you want to be—the past, present, or future. As you choose where you want to

---

[12] Seim Mol, "6 Major Companies That Failed to Innovate in Time," *GroundControl* (blog), October 7, 2020, https://togroundcontrol.com/blog/6-major-companies-that-failed-to-innovate-in-time/.

exist, that multiplies, making more of itself as it becomes so conditioned that it will be reality.

If you want to understand your current experience, you can get a sense of the sum total of your conditioning at that moment. Have fun knowing you're conditioning the forward pattern, so you can go all the way into your fullest, most complete reality.

Say Linda and Jack want to take their kids to Yellowstone National Park next summer. Both have happy memories of going there during their childhoods, and they want to carry this experience forward for Milo and Margot. They look at dates when they could go and plan road stops they could make along the way. They talk about the wildlife they will see and the cabin they get to stay in. Linda and Jack get to create this trip as the reality they want to experience.

Beyond planning fun activities, this patternshift is much more profound and far-reaching in its implications. That's because we are not just inhabitants of the planet—we *are* the planet. It is set up to go forward in a forward direction and for us to evolve along with it. This patternshift is allowing all of the future that is being given to you. So you're here to keep receiving the future, and that is the pattern. That replaces receiving the past.

You are always meant to receive your intended future. So receive it, and keep receiving it. You yourself are an evolution, and all of life is an evolution. An open, infinite field of possibilities is happening in this beautiful, forward-moving evolution and going with it, shaping it, as the future is being received by you, letting that future tell you what it wants to be. And also, you are telling it what it wants to be, too. This is all one symbiotic process. The gift of life is asking you to receive it every day. All of your intentions want to come to fruition through you, the co-creative vehicle that you are.

If you're unsure how to receive the future, don't overthink it. It is a combination of what you are feeling internally, along with information you choose to process from the outside world. For example, maybe your neighbor is sick, and you feel an internal pull to do something for him, but you don't know what is helpful. As you are driving, you pass by a farmer selling delicious roadside peaches. You pull over and buy some, and on your way home, you stop by your neighbor's house to drop the peaches off and say hello. You have co-created the future you wanted with the world, and it feels great.

The process of shaping evolution is one that humans are doing constantly, even when we're not doing a very good job at it. But think of how much more powerful this can be when you shape the future with intentionality instead of just reconditioning the past. Your reading this book is a deliberate, intentional way of shaping your future, and it is nothing short of a revolution. My team and I are a daily part of this revolution as well. The more people who read about this patternshift and learn to live in intentionality, the bigger this revolution gets, seamlessly creating more of itself.

What do you want the future to look like? Don't be afraid to dream big. In fact, whatever you think of, take it up a notch. Make it more fun, more glamorous, and better than you first thought. The future is asking you to shape it. It's asking you to say, "I want to feel like mint chocolate chip ice cream and sprinkles, million-dollar bills, hugs and kisses and foot rubs, luxurious blankets, and the perfect ocean view." Lining up with your best future is receiving and connecting to life. The forward pattern allows you to move beautifully through and with life. Thinking forward replaces the feeling that you have to go backward to fix things that are wrong in your life. You don't need to do that! Replace these "revisions" with your visions for the future.

Linda has a difficult relationship with her boss at work. She constantly feels she isn't doing enough. Linda tends to think about upsetting comments her boss made to her, and she ruminates about what she should have done or said instead. It's far more powerful for Linda to envision how she wants to feel at work—confident, heard, respected, and comfortable. As she holds on to this vision for her future, she handles herself differently with her boss. This transforms their work relationship—and Linda's self-worth.

Living forward allows you to receive all of the experiences you were encoded to receive. Forward motion advances your life so that every encounter with everything and everyone keeps getting better, easier, more beautiful, cooler, more efficient, more effective, simpler, more interesting, and more powerful.

You can see this through society's evolution. Even as we collectively perpetuate some past mistakes, there is also an undeniable momentum of forward progress. Medicine for chronic diseases is getting more effective, and cars are safer. You can instantly talk to someone on the other side of the world, thanks to technology. The speed of online information is lightning-fast.

PatternShift 5

When you connect to the energy of going forward, you find paradise on earth. That energy is also what is calling us to steward ourselves and to co-create with others. We are each meant to be in a powerful co-creating role. We are meant to know life more intimately and deeply, to know more of its beauty and artistry in its continual evolution.

This is an invitation to receive all of life and everything it's capable of being, everything that it is, and all of the potential it offers each and every moment. Decide to live in the now instead of in the past, and envision the future you want, focusing on that as your default state. When you do, you create a future with all your fellow co-creators in the Universe.

PatternShift 6

PROTECTION TO MOMENTUM

What do you think of when you hear the word "protection"?

Protection means preservation from injury or harm.[13] It can refer to many things, from condoms that protect against sexually transmitted infections and pregnancy to different types of insurance, such as health coverage or home insurance. Protection is also something we provide to those who are smaller or more helpless. Parents protect their kids from danger, for example, and the police are

---

[13] *Merriam-Webster*, s.v. "protect," accessed August 29, 2022, https://www.merriam-webster.com/dictionary/protect.

supposed to "serve and protect" law-abiding citizens from violent criminals.

Protection may conjure up feelings of safety, but in actuality, it isn't a preferred pattern. Protection operates from a very low frequency, and it implies we and others are not powerful or capable. It suggests that somehow we are weak and vulnerable. As such, it's an insidious pattern that is undesirable.

The idea of protection goes back to a time when the world was indeed a scary, dangerous place for humans. We were vulnerable to diseases, natural elements, wild animals, and other people who might cut our lives short.

According to the Centers for Disease Control and Prevention (CDC), life expectancy in the United States in 2020 was 77.8 years.[14] Much was made of the fact that this was the lowest number in the past twenty years. In fact, in 2019,

---

[14] Elizabeth Arias, Betzaida Tejada-Vera, and Farida Ahmad, "Provisional Life Expectancy Estimates for January through June, 2020," *NVSS Vital Statistics Rapid Release*, no. 010, February 2021, https://dx.doi.org/10.15620/cdc:100392.

life expectancy was a full year longer, at 78.8 years. This decrease in life expectancy is attributed to deaths from the COVID-19 pandemic, the biggest one-year dip since World War II (1942–1943).[15]

Nevertheless, living to nearly seventy-eight years of age is a vast improvement in overall survival rates. Although humans have been around for a few thousand years, even 160 years ago, life expectancy was merely 39.4 years.[16] Some people lived to become elders and grandparents, but far more people died young. Imagine thinking you might not even make it to age forty! And imagine fearing that your child might not live to see its first birthday. These were common concerns for the majority of human history.

Only in the last century and a half has life expectancy really changed, thanks to the advent of modern medicine, including

---

[15] Dania Nadeem, "U.S. Life Expectancy Falls to Lowest Level in Almost 20 Years Due to COVID-19—CDC," *Reuters*, July 21, 2021, https://www.reuters.com/world/us/us-life-expectancy-fell-year-half-2020-due-covid-19-cdc-2021-07-21/.

[16] Aaron O'Neill, "Life Expectancy (From Birth) in the United States, From 1860 to 2020," Statista, accessed August 29, 2022, https://www.statista.com/statistics/1040079/life-expectancy-united-states-all-time/.

vaccines.[17] Despite headlines we read in the news, in general, the world is safer now than in the past. According to Gallup's 2019 Law and Order Report,[18] a review of 140 countries shows the majority of people in the world feel safe walking alone at night where they live and have confidence in the police—that includes 85 percent of Americans. Of course, that means a significant minority of people still don't feel safe. This is especially true in war-torn countries such as Afghanistan and Venezuela.

Yet if overall we are safer than ever from the perils that afflicted our ancestors, why do so many constantly brace themselves for stress and danger? It's because thousands of years of running for protection is deeply ingrained and conditioned into us due to familial and societal history.

As the man of the family, Jack has been conditioned from a young age to believe it is his responsibility to protect his wife

---

[17] Regis College, "Public Health Initiatives and Life Expectancy: Immunizations," November 2, 2021, https://online.regiscollege.edu/blog/public-health-initiatives-life-expectancy-immunizations/.

[18] Julie Ray, "Most of the World Remains Confident in Police, Feels Safe," Gallup, October 27, 2020, https://news.gallup.com/poll/322565/world-remains-confident-police.aspx.

and children from harm. He works at a job he isn't passionate about because it pays well and he wants to protect his family financially. He installs a security system with cameras so he and Linda can monitor everything that's happening on their front porch and in the backyard. Jack feels pressure to keep a step ahead of everything, which can exhaust him and cause him to retreat from his family—the very people he is trying to help.

Linda, too, has been conditioned from childhood to live out the pattern of protection. She feels very protective of her children. Linda constantly keeps track of and monitors Milo and Margot—what they are eating, if they are sleeping enough, and how their moods are. She feels protective of her family as a whole. If anyone says something that could be construed as critical of Jack or the way they raise their kids, she gets angry and may even stop talking to that person.

There's so much conditioning around protection. How many times has someone said to you, "You have to protect yourself"? A very defensive pattern, protection is really a subpattern of attacking and fighting. When you think you have to defend yourself or others, you're not embodying your power as a creator of what you think, feel, believe, and act on.

PatternShift 6

Instead of protection, people really want their intentions to build momentum and manifest.

A lot of people say they want to be successful, but they are actually protecting themselves from success. The irony of protection is that it often keeps us from achieving the very things we want, even though we think protective measures will help boost success. If you want to accomplish something but repeatedly tell yourself you aren't good enough, you aren't giving it your all, because you are trying to shield yourself from having too much success—perhaps because of fear or doubt.

Let's say you know exactly what your dream job is, but you don't feel confident you can pursue it full-time. So you think you need to protect yourself from the risk of financial loss. So you work a mediocre job full-time and do what you really want as just a side gig. Or you take on two or even three other jobs so you will feel you have a safety net if your dream role doesn't work out.

Do you see what's wrong with this picture? It's a fear-based position. When your energy, time and intentions are spread all over the place, you can't make much momentum toward your goal. Of course you might need to save some money for a financial cushion, but the only way to achieve your intentions is to full-on focus on them. You have to plan to be a success instead of planning and living your life like you are going to fail.

What's more, this protective strategy is likely to cost you financially, even though that's what you're trying to avoid. When you aren't fully connected to what you are meant to bring forth in life, you deny yourself the chance to build the momentum of success, including monetary gains. This can actually equate to millions of dollars over your lifetime. All the influential individuals and golden opportunities you link to—and what they bring forth—would all create more of themselves. But when you don't allow that momentum to pick up speed, it's like putting a stopper in a bottle and then wondering why no liquid will come out.

Thus, you want to replace protection with momentum. When you have momentum in the pattern of what you intend, you are creating everything you want. You're creating reality, and you're receiving the energy and rolling with it. You are receiving all the momentum you're creating by focusing on it. That is a very, very beneficial pattern.

At his job, Jack has a habit of shutting down when he is around his coworker Jerry. They both have a similar rank in the company, but Jack has been there longer. He worries Jerry might get promoted before he does, thus denying him a coveted corner office and a raise. He is afraid Jerry will try to steal one of his ideas or use something Jack says against him, so he avoids talking to him whenever possible. Jack spends a lot of time and energy on "not Jerry," but a far more effective strategy would be to concentrate on himself and what he can do to earn a promotion. Getting a certification or taking on a new project would build the momentum to take Jack toward his true intention—to be valued and promoted at his company.

Momentum over protection is a very important pattern replacement, because when people feel they have to protect from something dangerous, it's usually because their true intention is to have the success they crave, to live their best life, and to feel happy.

The truth is, people aren't desiring to be protected from something they don't want in the first place. They don't want to be exposed to natural disasters, crime, financial ruin, or health problems. Living with that level of alarm of prospective or perceived danger is exhausting. All of your energy is sucked up just trying to survive, with no room to think about—let alone pursue—your intentions for a fulfilling life.

Even when you are protected from what you don't want, that doesn't mean you have what you *do* want. If you have flood insurance for your house, that doesn't mean you have the house of your dreams. It just means that in the event of a flood, you'll be reimbursed some costs of the damages to the house you currently live in. You are making a pattern of protection rather than a pattern of momentum, which is so powerful.

I'm not suggesting you should go through life with no protection. But think of protection as a direction you're giving to situations and events. When you wear sunscreen, you're creating healthy skin. To put up a baby gate is to direct your toddler where to play. Writing a will is intending where your assets will go.

Once you set up these sorts of practical protections, move on to spending the majority of your time and energy on your intentions.

Beyond that, look for patterns of protection in your life that unnecessarily cause you more stress than they are worth.

PatternShift 6

Remember that if you're planning on something awful, you will experience it, and it will confirm your bias and be validated, because that too has momentum—in the opposite direction of what you want.

Insurance companies are well versed in selling protection as a concept as well as a product. TV and online ads frequently emphasize the safety you will experience when you are a client of said insurance company. Or the ad might show a family that has escaped a car crash, calling its trusted insurance agent. These stories can be very convincing, appealing to our deep-rooted desires to protect ourselves and our loved ones from unexpected trauma.

Protection is about trying to guard against life and its villains. The problem with this narrative is that you don't want to be a victim! This line of thinking will not serve up the life you want.

Protection isn't just an outcome; as we talked about, it's a direction. Protection is a means to an end, to try to create an outcome. Give life an intention of the outcome you want so it doesn't have to guess or keep sending you in different directions. Be clear with the Universe about your ideal.

Ever since she can remember, Linda has wanted to travel to Greece. She loves going to Greek restaurants and has always enjoyed learning about the culture. She's watched the film *My Big Fat Greek Wedding* more times than she can count, and every day she posts a new picture of Greece on her Pinterest board. But she also spends a lot of time justifying why she can't go—the kids don't like long plane rides, and she and Jack are saving for a family trip to Disneyland. She feels she needs to put protection of finances ahead of her own intentions. So she resigns herself to planning a trip to Anaheim, California, where she doesn't even want to go, and it's a struggle for her to convey any genuine excitement about it to her family.

Having been an emotional scientist for a very long time—a person who studies the emotions of others—and a highly intuitive person, I know that people want life to work for them. They want to be in the flow, in the momentum. They want to have the wind beneath their wings. It's an amazing, forward-moving feeling.

When Linda gets into the flow of her intention to travel to Greece, suddenly a lot more possibilities open up. Her parents offer to take Milo and Margot to the beach during the summer, so she could go to Greece with Jack or a girlfriend during that time. She signs up for travel deals and finds an affordable flight to Athens that won't put a big strain on the family's Disneyland budget. She moves out of a pattern of protection into the realm of possibilities, making her vision of traveling to Greece a reality.

The same thing is available to you for whatever it is you're intending. You can have an amazing flow of energy toward anything you care about, like productivity and success. Receiving, intentionality, and momentum are the triple keys when it comes to going with life and creating with it.

When you're in that intentional momentum, you're very powerful. For the rest of your life, where you would have protected yourself—possibly from things you really want—you'll now have in its place the momentum of your intentions going forward toward what you want.

Starting now, you're following a new equation: the intention of momentum. Whatever protective patterns you have, replace them with your true intentions. Think to yourself, *What do I want this momentum to do? I want it to do this; I want it to do that.* Momentum is a great force of nature. It needs only your continual check-in: *Yes, keep going over there. Yes, upgrade that, please. Yes, I'll take more of that. Yes. Let's create some more of that.* That's how momentum works with your intention.

Move away from protecting yourself *out* of the life you want, and embrace the momentum of your true desires.

PatternShift 7

FICTIONAL TO FACTUAL

Here is an epic shift for an improved life: going from fictional to factual. This patternshift is key to a life in which you regularly navigate the facts of a situation to create the reality you want.

"Fictional" may not sound like the right term according to many of our beliefs. You may associate fiction with writers, or think it applies to people who struggle with delusions. But the dictionary definition of fiction is simply "something feigned, invented, or imagined; a made-up story."[19] And almost everybody makes up stories to some extent or another.

---

[19] Dictionary.com, s.v. "fiction (*n.*)," accessed August 29, 2022, https://www.dictionary.com/browse/fiction.

Emotionally sensitive people in particular can have many fictional ideas. That's because they are believing, absorbing, and experiencing a lot of stimuli, as well as communicating and expressing quite a bit. That can lead those who are sensitive to build up narratives and false beliefs that feel quite real. But anytime a person tells a story that isn't fact-based, that can create extra drama, which—you probably know what's coming—just keeps building more of itself.

When as children we didn't have the example of parents, guardians, or authority figures who operated in facts but spent a lot of time in drama, it can be difficult to learn to do this for ourselves. Like many people, Jack has fictional ideas from his childhood that he still believes today. As a boy, he was overweight and always one of the last kids to be picked for a team in gym class. Even now, he feels he isn't capable of being strong and fit, and he doesn't feel attractive. He has carried this shame for decades, even though it is not true. The facts are that he is healthy and enjoys running, and his wife finds him very attractive. And it's possible for him to become even more confident in his body if he chooses to challenge himself physically—and that's a fact.

To shift from being fictional to factual is a major upgrade.

PatternShift 7

As people tell themselves and others stories in which the narratives aren't based in complete factuality, falsehood creates more and more of itself. People can get so caught up in their version of a story that they actually start to believe it—but the facts don't change.

Let's say a coworker likes to embellish her versions of events to the point that you've learned to take anything she says with a degree of skepticism. She comes into the office late one day, and she's frazzled. She immediately tells you she just had *the worst time ever* at the pharmacy, trying to get a prescription refilled. The pharmacist was awful, the staff was rude and slow, and it all felt like a personal vendetta against her, she tells you.

Is this really the worst time your coworker has ever had in her life? Of course not. Service was probably slower than usual at the pharmacy, but beyond that, the pharmacy employees were not intentionally messing up her day. She made up this story because it reinforces her oft-repeated narrative that the world is against her. Her personalized fiction may cause her to act defensive and rude toward other people, so they reactively dish it back to her. Thus, her story continually creates more of itself.

It's no secret that politicians are masters of telling fictional stories, getting other people to believe them, and turning these fictions into bigger and bigger narratives that keep their constituents riled up. These fictional tales often have some facts at their core, but those are usually partial truths with plenty of drama layered on top. With the deep divisions in our political system, some politicians spend time "othering" people who don't agree with their policies. They build a narrative blaming the opposing party for our country's problems, taking a stand that no matter what the other party does right, they are still doing it wrong. The facts are that they are all part of the same political problems and trying to deal with the same issues. But it's virtually impossible to do so when each party has cast the other as morally contemptible, corrupt, and ineffective.

The problem with fictional ideas is that intentions can't work with them. *Intentions only work with facts*, so if you spend some or all of your time on fictional stories, you aren't focusing on your true intentions, so they are not likely to happen.

How do you strip away fictional and replace it with factual? Do it by looking at only the facts of a situation. Linda is convinced Jack is not in love with her anymore, because they were having a conversation about their anniversary party, and then he suddenly got in his car and drove off without a word. The only facts in this scenario are that he pulled out of the driveway and drove down the street. Her fictional story is that this action indicates he doesn't care about her. Perhaps he forgot to get milk at the grocery store, or he is going to pick up the dry cleaning before the cleaner closes. Until Linda knows exactly why Jack left, her best bet for staying with her intention of a strong marriage and family is to stick only to the facts of what occurred.

This patternshift is not just about the stories you tell yourself but also what you tell other people. If Linda calls her mom and complains that Jack doesn't care about her, her mother might get upset on her behalf because she doesn't want her daughter to get hurt. They might bring up incidents from years ago when Jack and Linda were dating, during which time they agree he acted thoughtlessly. Now Linda's mom is adding to the story, and probably creating some new stories as well, none of which help her daughter with her intentions.

The upgrade is that you've got to be able to tell yourself and others the facts, and to be consistent when speaking about your intentions. When you're operating in facts, you give yourself an emotional foundation for your intentions, which add up to your personal truth—the facts you want to be true.

Plenty of facts can feel painful, so at times it may seem more appealing to believe something that isn't fully true. But ultimately, it's still better to operate from the objective reality of a situation and then work from there.

Perhaps you had a beloved pet that quickly passed away following an illness. You don't want it to be true that your pet is no longer in the physical realm, but this is a fact. Living in the fictional story that claims you could have done something to prevent his illness only causes more suffering. The fact is that you had a wonderful pet for many years. Given this reality, you can intend to honor your pet by donating to an animal shelter or choosing a new pet in need of a loving home. Your intentions are up to you, and they are effective in achieving what you actually want, but only when you align with the truth.

These are some facts as I write this: It's seventy-five degrees outside. It's sunny. There are six clouds above. That's what's happening, and my intentions are the facts as I want them to be. I want it to be eighty degrees with clear skies for water-skiing on Memorial Day weekend. Those are the facts I want to occur.

When Memorial Day weekend rolls around, my intentions may manifest…or not. It might be pouring rain and fifty degrees. In that case I can tap into my underlying intention to have a fun weekend. My husband and I can choose instead to cuddle on the couch and watch movies. If I were to go water-skiing in the rain because I'm denying the facts of the weather, that definitely would not be fun!

Moving forward, choose to replace false stories with only the facts of a situation—the facts that are occurring and your desired facts, which are your intentions. So for the rest of your life, where there would have been fiction, you now know to focus on the facts. The facts provide your foundation for more intentionality toward the facts you want.

When Linda talks to Jack after he returns to the house, he confesses that he left because he felt overwhelmed with the party planning. He's not a fan of big events, but this has nothing to do with his love for his wife. Linda checks in with her intention, which is to have a fun party she and her husband will enjoy with close family and friends. She suggests they have a smaller party and she can plan it, no problem. This relaxes Jack and helps put him into the same intentions as Linda, and he offers to grill food and come up with a music playlist. Linda realizes all of the stories she'd fabricated about Jack's not caring about her were completely false, and she's glad she didn't accuse him of this as he walked through the door.

This is what I love about choosing intentions instead of reactions, as discussed in PatternShift 4, and how it relates to a factual shift. The facts of the matter could be that it's Saturday at five o'clock and you're wearing a blue shirt. And the facts you want intentionally are to put on a fancy outfit and go dancing at night. You have an infinite capacity to decide your intentions—the facts you want to bring to life.

Our intentions become facts when we are clear about, and in acceptance of, the facts occurring in the moment. So this is a huge upgrade—current facts get to drive our future facts.

What happens if you intend something for the future but it doesn't occur the way you wanted? Just keep sticking to the facts. Resist the urge to get pulled into a false narrative, like *Nothing ever works out for me*. Keep going to the facts.

The more you do this, the easier it gets and the more you align with the Universe's truth of your intentions.

Once you move away from fiction and into the facts of any given situation, you will be surprised at how liberating it feels. Too many people spend a tremendous amount of effort telling themselves and others stories that aren't true. Because these beliefs are false, they take a lot more effort to keep up with.

Milo and Margot decide they aren't doing their homework today, lying to their parents so they can instead go to the park and play. Milo tells his mom he already finished his math homework and that his sister finished her science project. Margot tells her dad she and Milo both wrote their English papers. It doesn't take long for their parents to figure out the inconsistency in their stories. Neither of them did any of their homework, and now they're busted for their lies. If the kids had stuck to the facts, they might have been able to negotiate doing their homework after a visit to the park. But as it is, they are both grounded and can't go to the park for the rest of the week.

Over a lifetime, we can accrue a lot of false stories. Some common ones are that we are not important, that we aren't talented, that nobody cares about us, that all of our value derives from some singular quality we have, that we are destined to have the same life as our parents and extended family, and that life is meant to be really hard. Those are just for starters!

When you feel a story swelling up inside of you, pause to examine its truth. Even when dealing with an emotional situation, look at it as if you're a fly on the wall. What is really occurring? What are you saying? What are you intending to happen? Many ordeals are often much simpler than they initially seem.

Moving from fictional to factual perspectives propels you that much faster into the life you intend. Do it every day, and you'll be in an elevated, highly intentional state most of your time.

PatternShift 8

PAIN TO PURPOSE

Replacing pain with purpose is a patternshift everyone in the world would want to make but very few people know how to do. I'm referring specifically to emotional pain, a pattern that is heavy in our atmosphere. In fact, it is perhaps the most widespread pattern in humanity.

Physical pain is very different from emotional pain. When a child scrapes their knee on the playground, they may wail and cry for a few minutes, and they might want a Band-Aid. But right away, their body starts the natural healing process without the child's needing to do anything. They quickly forget all about the scrape and get back to playing in the sandbox, moving on with life.

In contrast, emotional pain can hold people in a vice grip for a long time—even perhaps their whole lives. Emotional pain takes many different forms, from heartbreak to mental health struggles to habitual stress. Emotional pain might come from believing a host of horrible, negative things about yourself, other people, and the world. Emotional pain also comes from living in a society that is still very immature when it comes to making intentional training the utmost priority for a fulfilling life.

Many people have the ability to give birth to kids, and thus create life. But a lot of parents or guardians don't have a clue how to create productive, emotionally stable children. Most parents mean well and do their best given the emotional training they got as children, but that is often lacking. A lot of parents are told by relatives or friends to "figure it out" or "you know best" when, in fact, they are simply repeating old, broken patterns of pain that didn't work for them or the generations of their family before them.

When Linda was a little girl, her mom often made her feel

like she was eating too much. Linda got side-eye glances from her mother anytime she went for second helpings, and her mom would make a snide comment about "the Clean-Plate Club" when she finished all the food on her plate. Knowing how detrimental this was for her, Linda is careful not to treat her own children this way. But because she doesn't have a good barometer for how to teach her kids about healthy eating, she goes too far in the other direction. She offers ice cream or candy as bribes to get her kids to obey her, and she lets them eat any food they want in any amount. The pattern of broken eating keeps going in her family because of her own emotional wounds.

Pain is deeply conditioned into society, individuals, partnerships, collaborations, and companies. Every major religion preaches that suffering is an inevitable part of life, although they all have different ideas of how to handle it. But consider the idea that we have simply been taught this as part of our emotional training. Pain is an emotional pattern, just like being happy is a pattern. We've been given this fictional story that says pain is a requirement for life. But think about what it does to your psyche to believe this: *I'm alive, I'm going to be in pain*. How does this help you achieve a fulfilling life? Does it even make sense?

If you consciously or even subconsciously believe life is all about pain, then it will be. You'll suffer through it and have some moments of happiness along the way. This is terrible programming, that pain is the reality of our human condition. And it's only faulty emotional conditioning that promotes pain as this necessary experience everyone must suffer through.

No question, there is a tremendous amount of pain and suffering in the world. Famine, poverty, war, and disease cause physical and emotional strife. But emotional pain is not the only experience we encounter in life—it is one of many facets of the human experience, which also includes joy, belonging, peace, and purpose. All of these healthier patterns can be expanded upon. Pick your favorite—let's say joy—and think to yourself, *Since I'm alive, I'm going to experience joy!* You can feel lighter, just thinking this statement once. Imagine how much more elevated your life will be if you operate from this belief all the time.

Because the conditioning of pain is so pervasive, it comes with a lot of appealing PR. Having a high pain tolerance is a bragging right. Being a martyr is often revered.

But in reality, pain makes us crazy. It makes people lash out at one another, from small insults to the most horrible crimes. Emotional pain can torment people and even make them physically ill. Emotional pain spurs fights, yelling, domestic abuse, mass shootings, and other violent acts. It can cause heart attacks and contribute to autoimmune diseases. Some people turn to addictions, because they feel they have to check out when pain feels overwhelming. People in pain sometimes say awful things, especially to themselves.

Suffice it to say we all need this patternshift, big time. When you replace the pattern of pain with the pattern of purpose, you're taking all the energy that is hurtful and putting a new and purposeful shape to it.

When Linda taps into this purpose, she realizes she doesn't know how to eat sensibly because her whole model growing up was about limitation, which is more of a reactive form of direction instead of a positive, intentional one.

Linda can take the pain of being monitored and shamed for what she ate during her childhood and turn that into purpose, making sure her children understand the basics of healthful eating so they trust themselves to eat responsibly. Linda can go deeper into her purpose by taking a course on healthy eating and buying and cooking nutritious, satisfying foods for her family. From there, Milo and Margot can help her prepare meals so they start to learn how to do this, too. Linda's purpose can keep making more and more of itself.

When you're going into purpose, you're giving that painful pattern a new quality. It's like taking a basic staple such as dry pasta and then adding delicious sauces, cheese, vegetables, or meats in any combination that you want for a mouth-watering dish. Pain is a base emotional pattern, but through training, you can own your power and give your life purpose.

I did this process myself when my father passed away. I had a horrible, icky feeling of heartbreak, which can happen when struggling with pain. I decided my purpose would be about what I wanted to do with that pain. Purpose said to me, *If somebody dies and that's the worst pain I ever feel, then I can make it. I can take that purpose to make it so people learn to live fully through intentional training rather than die from emotional pain.* All of a sudden, I felt a shift in myself. I felt better, because purpose feels awesome. While pain is stagnant and keeps recycling, purpose gets you moving and feeling alive. Purpose elevates and inspires. When I made that shift, I became even more committed to my professional purpose.

To make a distinction about this process, a lot of times people try to make a purpose out of the pain itself. A person who was abused as a child might say, "Now I want to make it so nobody abuses anybody." But that purpose is about something *not* happening, which still highlights the abuse and makes it painful.

Purpose is better positioned toward a wholly positive intention. An example could be to intend that people purposefully treat themselves and one another with respect, cooperation, dignity, integrity, and love. Right there are five intentions that give purpose that much more energy. Intention drives the purpose forward, giving it direction and providing us with the actions and clarity to give momentum to the purpose. I want you—and everybody else—to have a healthy, pain-free sense of purpose for the rest of your life.

The everyday challenges of raising kids can be hard on Jack and Linda. They may lose sight of their purpose as a couple. As they get caught up in driving Milo and Margot to playdates, helping with homework, and shopping for back-to-school clothes, their marital intentions become neglected. But by tapping into purpose, they remember that their purpose as a couple is to support each other and have fun together. Jack and Linda can hire a babysitter for date nights a few times a month so they get to keep their intentions to each other. This strengthens their purpose to have a happy family as well.

Purpose is elevating, and it's our highest level. Every human being is here to live with purpose. You came into this world to create as many intentions as you can. This is how you contribute to society and to the world. When you operate on purpose—consistently ascertaining and following your purpose—your purpose keeps making more of itself and seeps into everything you do. When you get dressed, order groceries, or take out the trash, even all of those mundane tasks have purpose. When you take care of yourself or help another person, that's purposeful too. Your sense of purpose becomes a pattern that touches every aspect of your life. When you're in the momentum of purpose, you're right in the force of nature. Every interaction you have with yourself and others feels amazing when operating from this place of intention and drive.

Purpose can seem like a very heavy-handed concept with a lot of pressure to figure out what yours is. Some people feel they have to perfectly know their purpose, or their life isn't meaningful. Teenagers are often pressured to choose the "right" college major and then stay in the same job trajectory after graduating so they will make the most money. Society's attitude is often that a high-paying job (no matter how much you like it or don't) and being married with children are the only ways to live purposefully.

Even when you're a high achiever and capable of making any goal a reality, that doesn't mean a certain activity is necessarily your purpose. If you spend every weekend playing golf because that's what your peers do but your heart is really in nature photography, then you aren't living on purpose. You might feel like something is missing, or your mind might wander when you're teeing off. A lot of pain comes from following the prescription of what we're "supposed" to do with our lives, especially if that isn't compatible with who we truly are.

In reality, life and purpose are a lot less rigid than that. Purpose isn't a destination where you arrive at some mythical place and then never have to do anything else. Purpose is a journey you take throughout your whole life, and it often includes many twists and turns. If your purpose changes over time, that's okay—you evolve and change, and it's possible to amend your desires with the highest intention.

It's easier than it may seem to make the shift from pain to purpose. Ask yourself, *What's my purpose?* Focus on that question, and notice the answers that come up. In one moment, your purpose might be to make a delicious meal. In another it's to send a communication to facilitate an important career move you want to happen. Or your purpose may be to influence an amazing transformation in another human being through any number of co-creations.

I live out my purpose through intentional training. But there are countless ways to manifest purpose, because we are all unique. Maybe your purpose is to bake world-class cakes, or to transform young lives as a stellar parent or teacher. Your purpose on one day might be to build a great company, and the next day, it may be as simple as getting out to enjoy nature. Being in line with your purpose feels great, and it feels right.

Everybody naturally desires to have purpose in their life, so how great is it that purpose is available in every moment? From now on, whenever you feel pain or discomfort, replace it with the thought, *What's my purpose?*

It's okay to acknowledge your pain. But you can feel pain without getting wholeheartedly sucked into it. Purpose helps turn pain into productivity. And that is a really amazing and emotional process I invite you to partake in.

Like shifting fictional to factual, going from pain to purpose also has tremendous financial implications. People spend astronomical amounts of money on emotional pain, whether trying to escape it or acting out because of it. Junk food, alcohol, and cigarettes are just a few unhealthy habits people spend money on to distract themselves from painful emotions. If they stopped piling these metaphorical bandages on their pain, it would save them thousands of dollars.

When you're in a place of purpose, you also feel at peace. You don't feel the urge to buy items you don't need, because you're busy living your purpose and not filling your space up with superfluous stuff. It's like going from blurry vision to putting on a pair of perfectly precise glasses and seeing your life clearly. This trims away a lot of what isn't necessary, including how you spend money. And of course, as you keep living more and more on purpose, you'll undoubtedly make more money than you would have in a career that isn't your true calling.

The point of life isn't to be in pain—it's to live it on purpose, to set and live out your intentions in every moment. When

PatternShift 8

you stop falsely believing life is a painful slog to the grave and begin believing the truth that you are meant to feel joy, purpose, and peace every day, you'll create the very reality you want—or even better—on all fronts.

PatternShift 9

RELATIONSHIPS TO PARTNERSHIPS

No question, the pattern of relationships needs a major upgrade.

When I refer to relationships, that includes not only romantic connections but also the relationships between *all* the people on the planet—siblings, friends, lovers, neighbors, coworkers, and loads of strangers. Even when you drive, you have a relationship with the drivers and passengers in adjacent lanes, because you are sharing the road. We are always in relation to other people—that is a state of being. We also have relationships to objects, like money, and to elements of nature, such as the weather.

When a person says something like "I want a relationship with my mom," what they really mean is they want a more active, intentional relationship with their mother. The relationship is already there, even if it's not how they want it to be.

Relationships can be fraught with disappointment, stress, and dysfunction. We've been conditioned to believe relationships are inevitably hard. That belief creates a pattern through which difficult relationships keep perpetuating, and people remain passive recipients of these dynamics. Most people want to have better relationships with others, but many don't have any idea how to achieve this.

When we look at the pattern of relationships, we can see that the key concept to positively shift a challenging relationship pattern is for people to fully support one another as if they were in *partnership*.

Jack and Linda are each other's primary relationship. They are spouses, they are co-parents, they are lovers, and they are a family. They play many different roles together, but in their most elevated form, they are true partners. When they operate as a partnership, no one is keeping score of who last washed the dishes or whose turn it is to bathe the kids. Partnership is far more interesting, involving a shared vision for their life together.

At their core, Jack and Linda want to have a happy family. Of course, everyone wants this, and the challenge is figuring out exactly what this means for them and how they want to achieve it. For Jack and Linda, having a happy family means they both work from home so they can have a more flexible schedule to take their kids to and from school. It means they get takeout every Saturday night and watch a movie together as a family. And it means every summer they take the kids on a trip to a national park. Jack and Linda's partnership keeps them fueled through all of life's daily demands.

Your life is full of relationships, perhaps including a spouse and children. You might have siblings and cousins, your parents or stepparents, lots of friends, a few neighbors, and likely several coworkers. But the word "relationship" feels like a vague term for what people actually intend, which is to be in partnership with others.

PatternShift 9

Replacing relationship with partnership creates an entirely different level of reality. Partnership has a far deeper level of connectivity, activity, creativity, and intentionality.

In my years as a psychologist, speaker, author, and emotional scientist, I've seen that relationship issues are some of the greatest sources of people's emotional pain. A lot of this stems from how people *think* their relationship to a certain someone or something should be versus what it is. Maybe you think you should be closer with a friend you haven't seen in a few years, because you used to talk daily and you don't anymore. Or maybe you think your sister should mind her own business, but she's constantly asking about your marriage and offering unsolicited advice.

All of us have relationships with others that are less than ideal, and these can feel draining and disempowering. Shifting from thinking of these as relationships and instead approaching them as partnerships gives you a far more active role in the union—and helps you realize you and other people are together creating this dynamic.

Using the word "partnership" in place of "relationship" may not seem like a big distinction, but it is. Perceiving your interactions with another as a partnership takes you to the level at which you and the other person are collaborators. You're co-creators, and you're intending together. You're related to countless people in various ways, but that doesn't necessarily mean you're truly partnering, unless you take that intentional step.

Think about a marriage. For some people, marriage is basically like having a roommate with whom they have sex. They live in the same house, sleep in the same bed, parent the same kids, care for the same pets, and split up the household chores. But if you desire a true partnership with your spouse, you have to dig deeper than that—it's a lot more than having a marriage certificate you both signed. It's about sitting down together and discovering your shared intentions.

Partnership is an active co-creation that unfolds organically. It's about really being together and creating a reality together. And that is the same with anyone in your life—spouse, son, daughter, mother, father, brother, sister, cousin, aunt, uncle, friend, boss, coworker, dog, or even objects such as your car. You have many of these relationships and more. When you apply a partnering mindset to your primary relationships, an amazing upgrade takes place.

PatternShift 9

Some people feel the idea of partnership is too businesslike or formal, so they don't want to think of their personal relationships this way. But having a partner isn't a transactional relationship, unless that's what you want. With your husband or wife, you might say, "This is my partner in life." But the fact that you are actually creating reality together can get lost in the shuffle of the daily grind. You might feel like you're in a mundane relationship versus a genuine partnership with a shared set of intentions.

Creating intentions with others is the highest level of consciousness and capacity possible, because you carry those intentions out together and enter into a reality agreement. Partnership is the joint ownership of intentions.

So much falsehood is ingrained in us to expect relationships, including marriages and business ventures, to be difficult. "That's just the way relationships are," people might say. Maybe someone has told you, "Marriage is the hardest thing you'll ever do," or, "Parenting is the hardest thing you'll ever do." Does that sound like a great way to relate with the most significant people in your life?

Shifting to partnership also helps take out the adversarial

"other" pattern seen frequently in relationships. Relationships are often about mixing together the unique qualities each person brings, and this can be very positive. But it sometimes elicits a sense of hostility or competition between people. A relationship may have one person who is known for fun and spontaneity, while the other person leans toward being more responsible. If one person in a relationship is highly successful in a career, that can mean that the other by default is less of a success.

Partnership, on the other hand, takes you out of the competition realm and puts you and another person squarely in the reality of coexistence. You are literally creating the world together. You do this even with total strangers. If you are out walking and don't speak to a passerby, or they don't speak to you when you say hi, you're creating that reality together either way. So the partnership is real. And yet, you can shift dynamics to the level you want them to be by choosing partnership in all of your interactions. Partnership is your co-creative vehicle.

What might your life be like if, moving forward, you thought of every person you met as a partner? When you go to a restaurant, the server, the cook, and the rest of the staff are all partners in nourishing you with good food. This elevates your experience from a position from where you may not even pay much attention to the waitstaff to a purview of acknowledging the interdependence of all. You can partner with every person you encounter to better your life and theirs. Thank the busboy, smile at the hostess, and tip the server. Going to a restaurant now transitions from an ordinary occurrence to an extraordinary experience.

Those with the most intentionality get to create what they want. And that is available to anyone who is willing to be intentional and committed to positive outcomes.

Even with people in your life with whom you feel incompatible, think about what you do have in common with them and build a partnership from there. Or notice all the ways your differences are complementary. When you're driving, the person who cut you off in traffic is also trying to get home. Feeling that you're partners on the road can up-level your whole driving experience.

Jack and Linda sometimes operate as partners, and other times they fall into not-so-healthy relationship patterns in which they get caught up in what they "should" be getting from each other. Linda feels that since Jack is the man of the house, he should plunge the toilet when it gets clogged. Jack thinks that because Linda is a woman, she should fold all the laundry.

But when Jack and Linda perceive their union as a partnership, gender differences don't matter so much. They are partners in running a home together, creating a reality that includes every single outcome that represents their life's intentions.

When they amicably discuss issues and focus on creating their desired outcomes—a clean home; clean, ready-to-wear clothes neatly folded in the drawers; and a refrigerator full of food to nourish their family—then their collaboration takes on a creative quality. The couple's desired outcomes are accomplished because they are shaping their reality together instead of fighting over the to-do list. When they create together with a strong connection to the outcomes instead of the process, the inspiration comes easily for them to create those outcomes.

In every instance where there would have been just a relationship, you're now invited to turn toward partnership.

PatternShift 9

Every day is an opportunity to live in partnership with people. Now all of your intentions are a partnership, either between yourself or with another person. All of the encounters you have with people in the world, in life, around you are partnerships. From now on, all relationships you have with anything or anyone can be consciously replaced with partnerships, and you'll see that these deeper connections will keep becoming exponentially more substantive.

Operating as partners makes it so you and another person upgrade as co-creators and collaborators. You're partners in creating reality and materializing shared intentions. It's phenomenal.

And you can expand on your intentions to step into healthy partnerships by reevaluating your current relationships not only with people but also with things—like partnering with money, partnering with resources, partnering with finances, or partnering with materials in the world, like the carpet you select for your home. If you whittle a piece of wood into a statue, you're partnering with the wood to give it shape and beauty it is not capable of forming on its own—you and the wood are in partnership for realizing potential.

PatternShift 9

So this language, this conversation, this discussion, this consciousness, this conceptualization—it upgrades everything. Partnership allows you to perceive the truth of a person, to identify any unhealthy relationship patterns running and then replace them with positive intentions. Partnership promotes intentionality. The partnership can do this because everybody involved with it knows that it's *their* partnership. People put into a partnership—and into its matrix—what they want it to be rather than judging it for what they *don't* want it to be.

Don't worry about how you think your relationship with someone should look. Work with the facts. As with shifting from fictional to factual patterns, your intentions are effective only when you focus on the fact that you are in partnership with each other. Focus on creating shared desires within a reality where all intentions can coexist harmoniously.

Partnership is a creative framework and identity mechanism that is effective and productive. This will likely be a paradigm shift for you as you move forward in a patternshift to replace relationships with partnerships in every instance. For the rest of your life, where you would have had a base relationship, you now choose partnership with everyone and everything in the world—and with yourself.

PatternShift 9

Although partnership is typically thought of as engagement with other people, note that your connection with yourself is the ultimate partnership. Partnering with yourself means keenly listening to your inner navigation and deliberately setting your intentions each and every day. Partnering with yourself allows you to manifest your desires through intention, which is heightened by making conscious shifts and upgrades to relationship patterns. When you have a successful partnership with yourself, you're able to partner with other people that much better. Partnering with yourself means truly listening to your inner navigation and setting your intentions, each and every day.

Of course, it's also possible to partner with more than one person. When groups of people share the same intentions and work together to make them happen, possibilities are limitless. You can see this with great companies, where all of the employees work toward shared goals and innovations. Partnerships are also forged with families, sports teams, communities, religious groups, or even whole countries. Such partnerships are highly successful, provided the sincerity of intentions stays consistent and people don't get mired in relationship hang-ups.

In reality, you are intentionally partnering with people across the world. It's about recognizing that we are all in partnership —humans and every other species. We are a beautiful ecosystem of partners in this reality, and our partnership lends itself to the highest, most elevated state of being.

You're now welcome to fully join this universal partnership. You're welcome to inhabit it, embody it, live it, and experience it in all its potential.

PatternShift 10

SCARCITY TO LUXURY

When you think of the word "luxury," what comes to mind? Are you at a fancy beach resort, sipping on a cocktail? Are you in a penthouse suite in Las Vegas, getting ready to hit the town?

Or are you simply in a comfortable home with plenty of food to eat, knowing you'll never again worry about money?

Luxury can mean something different to everyone. That's part of what makes this patternshift so much fun—it's all about what you can dream of, aspire to, and achieve. The world is full of luxury, even though a tremendously significant amount of the population is in a mindset of scarcity.

Shifting from scarcity to luxury is an absolute transformation for people because scarcity is such a pervasive emotional pattern in humanity, one that supports a perceived absence of material outcomes. Scarcity indicates a *lack* of something.

People who live in a scarcity mentality may think money is their biggest concern, but this programming affects every aspect of their lives. They feel they are strapped for resources and for time and often feel lacking in love as well.

Scarcity is an emotional programming matrix that appears to keep people in poverty. And scarcity doesn't affect only those who seem to lack money. Having worked with some of the wealthiest people on the planet, in an echelon of true riches, I can tell you that the scarcity program can exist in the heart of someone who has $280 million. That scarcity mindset makes even millions of dollars feel like it's not enough, as if the bottom might fall out at any moment.

Scarcity leads to material and experiential outcomes, and I consider it one of the more dangerous elements in the human psyche. Replace scarcity with luxury because in the evolution of humanity, wherever there has been an experience of lack—when people were legitimately hungry and starving—we can look at it and acknowledge, yes, that's what occurred. But that was a situational reality and not a permanent state. And some of this lack came from a scarcity mindset as well. Through the course of human evolution, intentionality—even if not deliberately applied—activated a new reality, such as learning to grow crops so there would be enough food.

Scarcity conditions a perception that says the world is empty and always will be: *there isn't enough to go around, and we're out of what we need.* This misinterpretation of reality is so ingrained that this perception of scarcity remains even though our world has more excess than ever. We have more resources, food, and medicine to keep everyone healthy, even if access is still a problem for some—which can also be shifted through intention.

Jack's grandparents grew up during the Great Depression, and he keenly felt this as a child whenever he visited their home. They bought the most inexpensive foods at the grocery store and rarely dined out. His grandparents frequently complained about the rising prices of just about anything, from gasoline to shoes. He got the distinct impression they were poor, and he was shocked after they passed away to learn they had been quite financially well-off. He felt sad that they didn't spend their money at all on entertainment or travel or other luxuries while they were alive to enjoy it.

While there are plenty of people like Jack's grandparents, not everyone functions this way. A certain segment of the population believes in luxury, creativity, and innovation, and they are constantly creating. They follow through with intentionality to be in a continuous emotionally luxurious state. When they want to create something new, they do it. And they just keep on creating.

Scarcity mindset is a negative pattern, the false belief in lack. If, say, there were ten people and two pieces of candy, an intentional conversation would focus on appreciation for the candy. The scarcity conversation would bat around the idea that there isn't enough candy to go around for everybody. Scarcity's very interpretation explains what *isn't*, and the continuous process of doing that keeps the misperception of lack looping—more of itself in all different forms as represented in the scarcity pattern.

When someone is struggling financially and has trouble putting food on the table, they are deep in the belief that there isn't enough. A luxury mindset is to look at the excess available in the world and think, *I'm going to receive this excess—that's my focus and my destination.*

Putting luxury in place of scarcity says, *That's mine, too. Those are resources I will engage in and share, because the world is full of resources.*

People who live in a state of luxury can keep creating house after house, boat after boat, car after car, record after record, fashion line after fashion line—they are just in the pattern of continually creating. And that luxury is a far more powerful pattern than scarcity. Replace the scarcity pattern with luxury, and hold your focus to have anything you need at every stage of life and under any circumstances.

Luxury entails having the money to choose, create, and acquire *anything*. Humans are living their full potential when in a state of luxury, having an all-access pass to unlimited choices. The ability to deliberately move from intention to creation is a very high level of mastery, and money is a representation of conscious intentionality. Money is a currency—

a current of energy—that provides a material means by which we can achieve much in this world.

This shift from scarcity to luxury can be challenging, because many people have been passed down a scarcity mindset from their families for generations. Some might not even know what luxury is supposed to feel like, because they are so used to struggling financially. My sense of luxury is about feeling the most comfortable experience of life, a deep relaxation of living in my power without feeling a need to be forceful.

Luxury is a state of relaxation that understands that your intentions, along with everyone else's, create reality from the moment you connect with them and in all the moments you choose to be in line with them. If other people are in a scarcity thought process, your intentional responses can influence them toward luxury, too. Essentially, whatever is being thought, felt, or spoken by everybody is co-creating reality. So it's that much more important to connect into the deep luxury of being.

Until track-and-field athlete Carl Lewis broke a world record in 1991, it was widely believed that human beings weren't capable of running the one-hundred-meter dash in less than ten seconds.[20] But Lewis ran it in less than ten seconds because he didn't subscribe to the old belief. He chose to believe he could outrun current times, and this helped him condition his body into being the vehicle that created that reality. And now we have constructed a new reality, which is that humans are better, stronger, and faster.

Today, instead of playing a vinyl album, I click on my phone's keypad to hear my favorite song. In fact, now I have the whole world at my fingertips, thanks to my phone, because that's the reality that was conceptualized and then constructed. This level of unprecedented media access elevates all of us, allowing us to communicate, research, and store information in ways that were unthinkable to many of our ancestors. With one click, I can order just about anything I want shipped to me.

When many of our grandparents wanted to learn about a topic, they went to their local library and checked out a book or researched it on microfiche. They were limited by whatever

---

[20] World Athletics, "Athlete Name: Carl LEWIS," accessed August 29, 2022, https://worldathletics.org/athletes/united-states/carl-lewis-14244008.

resources were available at the library at the time. If a book was checked out, they lacked that information until the book was returned. Now, Jack can use his phone to Google any subject matter and be referred to hundreds of sources within seconds. We all benefit from this level of sophistication.

Those who live in the mindset of luxurious reality get to experience it tangibly. This is true whether or not the pattern of luxury was passed down through multigenerational creation or if somebody newly engages with and embraces the luxury pattern—maybe even gets obsessed with luxury and becomes one with it.

Luxury is available to *everybody*, and if you're ready to travel the distance, know that it's an internal journey. The intentional training process helps you make that shift, using the power of your imagination. Listen to your navigation and decide what luxury you want to create, what you are here to create.

Let me reemphasize that, like all of the shifts featured in this book, luxury is ultimately an inner state of being. While it has many outer representations—money, jewels, fancy cars, fine wines—luxury is a reflection of how you feel inside.

When referring to how much money a well-off person has, some might say, "Well, they are really comfortable." That feeling of luxury and ease is natural. If you take the opposite, that means people are uncomfortable. When I study this from my perspective as an emotional scientist, I see what the conditioning of scarcity does—it creates a continuous experience of discomfort, even if relative to specific moments and situations.

But the pattern of luxury is continuous as well, creating all facets of itself, both material and experiential. Relaxation derives from the ability to create anything, to have whatever you need and want and love, to purposefully go from an intention to a luxurious outcome. And honing that ability to infinitely create in any given moment, no matter the circumstance or associated factors, is the ultimate in achieving a state of absolute certainty. It's a fabulous and wonderful level of comfort to achieve.

A comfort exists when you know you can experience life in emotional and material luxury, regardless of what's going on in the world's economy. Many people live in luxury despite bleak economic setbacks or forecasts. This can lead to a lot of frustration, anger, or desperation in someone who is in the scarcity mindset. A scarcity-minded person might feel envious or be resigned to the idea that they never have luxury.

But if you keep focusing on the world's natural abundance and all that's available, you get more and more in tune with luxury. Focus on the abundance of wealth, riches, comfort, safety, happiness, certainty, beauty, and texture—as one would say, the world is your oyster. Not just through your smartphone, but, literally, what your imagination can create. The possibilities are boundless, and knowing you can freely tap into this state is very comforting and relaxing.

The vision of all-encompassing, full, multidimensional wealth looks different for everyone—this house or that house or no house, traveling the world, or giving everything you own to charitable causes you love. Whatever your preferences, you are able to create anything you intend, including the accumulation of money.

A lot of people want to live in luxury, and they might occasionally think about what it would be like to drive the car they really want or wear designer clothes, but they don't get very far. As we've discussed, physics doesn't allow the concept of *I'm going to do something else and then hope that this other experience happens*, and it will take potentially forever. Without consistency, shifts can take generations to achieve, making very slow strides amid unnecessary struggles.

So this is an important shift. Intentionality cuts through all of that and shrinks the effort. We don't need generations to pass before one family system finally, all of these many years later, sees its first family member go to college, have a lucrative career, and hold an affluent position. It's not necessary. Instead, be in the focus of intentionality, in the focus of luxury, and attract to yourself like a money magnet every dollar decimal point you want.

Having done intentionality training for years, I can attest that intentionality is paradigm-shifting, creating an entirely new chain of events aligned with intentional reality over reactive reality.

Surround yourself, whenever possible, with people who know, live, and breathe material luxury from their emotional core. You can rise above the lower-vibration consciousness of others. If everyone you know is in the scarcity mindset, turn to more positive influences by listening to talks from successful people, reading books written by affluent authors, or joining a local entrepreneurs' group. Network with luxury-minded people.

When you create that much more luxury conditioning, you experience its benefits and build from even more luxury. Your example of living in luxury helps others make the transformation, not only materially but also from the deepest emotional level. Luxury is continuous, lasting, resonating, and adding to the greater good, a very important service to this world.

If this sounds like a pipe dream—if you think, *Not everyone can be rich and successful. There always have to be a few people on top and everyone else down below them*—know that the physics don't bear this out—they don't support your doubt.

What you focus on, you create more of. So as you create more money and resources, you're doing this in addition to what already exists. You don't have to take something away from someone else in order to be a success. There's no reason to fear enormous success and luxury.

I invite you to make this shift from scarcity to luxury. Every time you perceive scarcity, replace it with your vision of luxury, and feel that in every level of yourself. Luxuriate (pun intended) into how fabulous that feels and what all of it entails. Construct it and give it numbers and texture: how luxury feels and what it looks like in your mind, where your primary residence and other properties are ideally located, your dream vacation destinations, high-end shopping sprees and spending excursions, planned investments, favorite five-star restaurants.

Scarcity has such a deep impact on people, especially as related to money, which is where people struggle most with this conditioning. Intentionally choose luxury, and hang out there permanently. You can live it, breathe it, and say it, over and over—luxury. All of your previous money conditioning —the stories falsely patterned around lack of money and limited resources—can be fully replaced with the truth of limitless luxury and excessive resources here in this world for everyone to receive. They are there; they are yours. A firm belief in your worthiness and ability to live luxuriously allows you to receive and steward luxury. Go ahead, and create everything you want. Just use your imagination.

Conclusion

We are all made up of myriad patterns. There are as many patterns as there are human beings in the world. As you've probably come to realize, there are far more than only ten patterns that most people could benefit from shifting.

But you're also probably getting a sense of how optimal patternshifts work. They are all about steadily moving forward in intention and living with a deep sense of joy and purpose. They are about rejecting the status quo and instead being profoundly in tune with your Self and the unique contributions you're here to make in the world. And they are about embracing life, with all of its

Conclusion

flaws, and focusing on what works and what you want to develop more of.

Because you're human, you may sometimes find yourself slipping back into old patterns. This tendency occurs because you're surrounded by reactivity every day and because you're transforming decades and sometimes even millennia of human conditioning. Don't be hard on yourself. You're going for progress, not for perfection.

As you live more and more intentionally, you will find it easier to acknowledge when you're in a pattern that isn't serving you, and you'll be better able to shift into what you want that much faster.

And as you master your own patternshifts, you'll look around at other people with amusement as you watch the same patterns we've discussed in this book crop up over and over. You'll notice people who are largely unconscious of themselves, stuck in fearful patterns of negativity and isolation, living in the past. You'll pick up on the false stories people tell themselves and others about their lives. And you'll see how few people, even married couples, function as true partners.

Conclusion

Instead of feeling discouraged by all of these broken patterns, put on your emotional scientist hat. Observe them objectively, and then you can help change the other person's life by simply asking, "What's your intention?" or "What do you want in this situation?"

Most people are not used to thinking in terms of what they actually want. They are used to reactivity, confusion, and negativity, with some unconscious intention thrown on top.

But when you live with conscious intention and inspire others to do the same, you're evolving the world in a positive way. You're busting through all of that old, tired conditioning and creating a new reality—one that we all sorely need, starting immediately.

Thank you for your willingness to take a clear look at yourself and the patterns that shape your life. And thank you for joining me on this revolutionary ride to a better, more intentional you—destined to bring exactly the gifts you're meant to contribute to our human family.

Keep shifting your personal patterns, and the world's, and you'll do everything you've ever dreamed…and more.

Further Resources

As you continue to recognize and shift the patterns that you want to upgrade, you may find that making internal changes is much easier with additional strategic support.

This support can come from the people in your life who know and love you, who are familiar with your patterns and are going to be some of the greatest beneficiaries of these positive shifts.

But for many of us, the people we're close to have plenty of patterns of their own that need shifting. That's to be expected. However, as we talked about in Chapter 10, it's very important to surround yourself with people who are in a luxury mindset instead of a scarcity one. Intentionality is what makes this possible.

To surround yourself with the very best and reach this state of pure intentionality, I highly suggest visiting my company's website: https://www.theempirecompany.com/.

There, you'll find a wealth of resources (pun intended) to help make patternshifts with lightning speed by working with me and my talented team of transformational directors who specialize in coaching highly successful people to become their top Selves. As the name implies, The Empire Company turns businesses into empires, families into dynasties, and individuals into moguls who live out their destiny.

Whatever your dream, whatever patterns you wish to shift and elevate, The Empire Company can help.

The simplest, most effective way to get started—or just talk to us about your goals—is by booking a consultation call with a member of our world-class team. The information on how to do so is on our website.

Further Resources

This is a no-cost, thirty-minute call that will help you reveal the most profound patternshifts you can make and give you a plan to get there. It's an intention session to assess how we can help you best.

Now let's shift you into the life you've always wanted.

With love and intention,

Dr. T

Acknowledgments

I'd like to start by acknowledging one of my favorite people in the universe, Director Christa Dordal, for being such an exceptional patternshifter and making her own brand of Christa Magic. Her ability to transform some of the most difficult human patterns like scarcity into the most incredible reality of luxury for so many people is truly world class. At The Empire Company, Director Christa is a role model for so many as she takes total responsibility for creating intentional reality, no matter what she absorbs from the outside world. She's in a class all her own as a phenomenal, transformative leader that goes all in building the most intentional reality for her incredible Dordal Empire Family, as well as our Mogul-Making, Reality-Creating Family at The Empire Company.

Acknowledgments

Director Christa has shifted every kind of negative pattern ever put in her path and elevated herself into one of the most luxurious people I've ever encountered. To witness her is to witness one of the greatest lifestyle artists on the planet. She is so aligned with The Empire Company's core Method of patternshifting negative emotions into positive intentions, and she has become truly masterful in it, creating upgrades wherever she goes. She beautifully receives every shift and has fun with it, which means the world to me because life is so fun, and more than anything, I live for people to have fun with creating reality.

It is Director Christa's playfulness and the world's most beautiful smile on her face that truly transform me and everyone who has the gift of her presence. The sense of humor that she and I share gets both of us laughing hysterically, and I love to see "DC" crack up at the silliest shifts I send her way. Director Christa represents all that The Patternshift makes possible for people as someone who has elevated herself into full mogul status, is operating in a power-couple mode with her mogul partner, Erik, and is leading an Empire Family as she and Mogul Erik empower their sons and daughters into Purposeful Moguls who are all stewarding the Dynamic Dordal Dynasty together.

Acknowledgments

Director Christa and her partner, Mogul Erik, are quite simply super role models for society. It is because of their commitment to living intentionally and to living out their humanitarian purpose with every shift they make that they are the architects of one of the great American Dynasties. Director Christa and Mogul Erik live out what it means to be citizens of the world and brother and sister to the entire human family. They have it all, they know it, and they share it, and that is my definition of a Dynasty.

To acknowledge Director Christa in the entirety of what she means to me and the world at large for all that she has done to embody intentionality is to give her the highest compliment I can give anybody, and that is to say that she is family. She is family to me because she is family to everybody, and that is the greatest shift a person can make. It is getting to be a humanitarian family with Director Christa and our shared definition of family. That is a luxury that I wish for everybody.

I also want to acknowledge all the people in my life who have helped me shift to a higher level of my Self through their actions and words of wisdom—the people who have cared about me, invested in me, and who helped me upgrade into my most intentional Self. That includes my big, blended,

Acknowledgments

extended family; my friends, both long-term and new; and all they've brought that has allowed me to live my purpose and have a very fabulous life.

In addition, I want to acknowledge my friend Deanna Madson Shaat, whom I've known since the age of five. She's been with me almost my whole life, allowing me to so fully be me in my most elevated, happiest, hilarious Self. Deanna is my greatest audience ever. She's so open for me to make her laugh to the point where she can barely breathe—that's how willing she is to receive. And she's willing to have so much fun in life, including all the ways we both make fun of what it is to be a human and we crack each other up. Deanna makes me the most fun version of myself, the Lucille Ball version, performing physical comedy, dialing it up until we're both bellyaching with laughs and knowing that we can both go for hours finding the fullest level of funny and squeezing every laugh out of any situation. When I was little, I realized that I could make Dee laugh, and I felt so much better about myself, and for the rest of my life, making Dee laugh is one of my most important contributions to society.

There are plenty of people who are willing to be there in times of struggle, and yet someone who will laugh with you

Acknowledgments

at every turn is incredibly valuable to me for my own sake and for the purpose that I live out each day. Deanna has literally laughed at every joke I've ever made to her, and that makes her someone I can depend on for the thing that I love the most, which is laughter. Deanna is the center of my lifelong friend group from those early times in my life, and she makes life feel luxurious because laughter is what bonds us the most. Not only has she contributed to my well-being but also to countless transformations of everyone who has ever been in contact with me, because she is a foundational aspect of my life and she both encourages me and expects me to turn life's tragedies into comedy for her amusement, and that has made all the difference. I don't know who I'd be if I had to settle for the tragedy that I've experienced around me throughout my life, and with Dee as my friend, I've always had a way to make things better because I could make her laugh out loud in the queue and she always plays along. It is Dee's laughter and her capacity for joy that has made her a most treasured lifelong companion.

In the creation of The Patternshift, it's important that I acknowledge a dear friend, Stacy Leibowitz, whom I met while living in Manhattan. Stacy quickly became an essential

Acknowledgments

friend as she brought a rock-solid foundation to the intensity of living in New York. Stacy is a soul-family sister to me because at the core she is a compassionate humanitarian and a naturalist who cares deeply for all living beings. She's an inspiration for how to live in harmony with all creatures and to honor all of creation as divine. Stacy is a stunning person who brings so much to people's lives, and she does this without realizing how magnificent she is and how the gift of her friendship feels like having a trillion dollars in the bank.

I love Stacy for so many reasons, and I am able to live out my purpose because she's in my corner. Stacy celebrates me for who I am and also for who I am able to be in any given moment, and she has supported me in what I care about the most, which is elevating humanity into intentionality. She is ever-present with me while being 3,000 miles across the country, and she provides a deep sense of peace in the knowledge that she understands me and loves me anyway! To boot, she is funny as hell and has a beautiful balance of deep compassion and making fun of life with me, because we can scratch our heads together as we contemplate the interesting journey of reality and observe the bewildering humor of human behavior.

Acknowledgments

I'd also like to acknowledge all the other friends I've had, from different regions of the county and different parts of my journey, who have loved and laughed with me. All of these kindred spirits that have ever contributed a chat, a phone call, an email, a text, hangout time, a smile, a tip: they've helped me every step along the way to be the person to live out my purpose in bringing advancing intentionality in our society. I am fortunate to have so many great friends who have contributed to my life and helped me create an intentional reality that supports so many people every day.

The same acknowledgement goes out to The Directors of Reality at The Empire Company and The Dynasty Company. I want to acknowledge every contribution, every patternshift, and every upgrade that everyone on our Reality Team has made to make our most intentional reality of luxury that we share with society.

And to our clients, who are our incredible partners in intentional reality creation, they deserve tons of credit for all the shifts they make happen. An acknowledgement for all they do to make an elevated reality possible for everyone in their companies and their families, creating it forward for generations to come. We are collaborators together pioneering

Acknowledgments

the intentional reality of luxury, and each day they powerfully transform into incredible moguls of great empires and dynasties.

Always and in all ways, I deeply acknowledge our fans and audience who connect with us through our media network, following us implementing every patternshift we provide each day. I am so grateful that they receive the gift of these upgrades and install them into their lives with the joy and fun that is intended for them. Thanks to them for joining our flow and helping us make the world a more luxurious space.

www.ingramcontent.com/pod-product-compliance
Lightning Source LLC
Chambersburg PA
CBHW070140080526
44586CB00015B/1778